THE PEACH {
100 DESTINATIONS YOU MUST VISIT

GEORGIA

─ TRAVEL GUIDE ─

DIANA L.
MITCHELL

Table of Contents

I

II

III

Dear reader, thanks a lot for purchasing by

To help you plan your trip even more efficiently, I have included an interactive map powered by Google My Maps.

To access it, scan the QR code below.

Happy travelling!

A Note to Our Valued Readers

Thank you for choosing this travel guide as your companion for exploring the world.

I want to take a moment to address a concern you might have regarding the absence of photographs in this book.

As an independent author and publisher, I strive to deliver high-quality, informative content at an affordable price.

Including photographs in a printed book, however, presents significant challenges. Licensing high-quality images can be extremely costly, and unfortunately, I have no control over the print quality of images within the book.

Because these guides are printed and shipped by Amazon, I am unable to review the final print quality before they reach your hands.

So, rather than risk compromising your reading experience with subpar visuals, I've chosen to focus on providing detailed, insightful content that will help you make the most of your travels.

While this guide may not contain photos, it's packed with valuable information, insider tips, and recommendations to ensure you have an enriching and memorable journey.

Additionally, there's an interactive map powered by Google My Maps—an essential tool to help you plan your trip.

I encourage you to supplement your reading with online resources where you can find up-to-date images and visuals of the destinations covered in this guide.

I hope you find this book a helpful and inspiring resource as you embark on your next adventure.

Thank you for your understanding and support.

Safe travels,

Diana

Introduction

Welcome to *Georgia Travel Guide* — your ultimate guide to exploring the rich diversity of destinations in the Peach State. From the bustling streets of Atlanta, where modernity meets Southern charm, to the tranquil beauty of the Blue Ridge Mountains, this guide is a treasure trove for travelers seeking both iconic landmarks and hidden gems of Georgia.

Our journey begins in Atlanta metro area, a region pulsing with cultural vibrancy and historic significance. Stroll through the expansive grounds of the Mercedes-Benz Stadium or catch a thrilling game or concert at State Farm Arena. Dive into the history of college football at the College Football Hall of Fame or relax in the green expanse of Centennial Olympic Park. Each destination, from the world-renowned Georgia Aquarium to the historic Martin Luther King Jr. National Historic Site, offers a unique slice of the city's dynamic offerings.

As we venture south, we'll explore the rich tapestry of Coastal and Southern Georgia. Marvel at the antebellum architecture of the Savannah Historic District and step back in time at Fort Pulaski National Monument. Southeastern Georgia melds history, culture, and natural beauty, with highlights like the serene Jekyll Island Historic District and the adventurous allure of the Okefenokee Swamp.

North Georgia and the Mountains beckon with their natural splendor and artistic charm. Be inspired by the creative retreat of Helen Alpine Village or indulge in the local flavors with a tour of Georgia Wine Country in Dahlonega. This region is a haven for art, nature, and history enthusiasts, offering attractions like the panoramic Brasstown Bald and the tranquil trails of Smithgall Woods State Park.

Finally, our exploration extends to Central and Eastern Georgia, where history permeates the charming towns and vibrant cities. Walk the historic campuses of the University of Georgia in Athens, enjoy a reflective moment at Ocmulgee Mounds National Historical Park in Macon, or embrace the natural beauty of Callaway Gardens in Pine Mountain. This region is steeped in historical significance and bursting with cultural activities, from museums to music venues.

Georgia Travel Guide is more than just a travel guide; it's an invitation to experience the diverse beauty, history, and culture of Georgia. Each of these destinations has been carefully selected to offer you an authentic and memorable journey through the Peach State. So pack your bags, bring your curiosity, and get ready to explore Georgia like never before!

About Georgia

Landscape of Georgia

In *Georgia Travel Guide*, we delve into more than just the places; we explore the very canvas upon which these destinations are painted – the varied and enchanting landscape of Georgia. This chapter introduces the diverse terrains and natural wonders that make Georgia a miniature representation of the Southeast's natural beauty.

Coastal Elegance: Beaches and Marshes of the East

Eastern Georgia is renowned for its scenic coastline. From the historic Savannah waterfront to the pristine beaches of the Golden Isles, the eastern edge of the state presents a dramatic intersection of land and water. The coast is adorned with iconic lighthouses like Tybee Island Light, standing as beacons of maritime heritage. The influence of the Atlantic Ocean shapes the unique culture of these coastal areas, where fishing and maritime traditions are deeply ingrained.

Urban Green Spaces and Rivers

The urban landscapes of Atlanta and Savannah are skillfully woven with green spaces. Piedmont Park in Atlanta and Forsyth Park in Savannah offer serene retreats within these bustling cities. The Chattahoochee River, flowing through the state, provides a picturesque setting for urban adventures and is a favored spot for rafting, fishing, and riverside gatherings.

Mountains and Valleys: The Northern Highlands

Northern Georgia is marked by the majestic Blue Ridge Mountains and fertile valleys. This region boasts a tapestry of small towns, sprawling forests, and rustic charm. The autumn foliage here is a spectacle, with vibrant colors transforming the landscapes into a canvas of red, orange, and yellow. The area is also home to rivers and mountain streams that offer a plethora of recreational opportunities.

The Historic South: Plains and Agricultural Landscapes

Central and southern Georgia feature historic plains and expansive agricultural lands. This area includes places like the antebellum homes of Macon and the sweeping fields of the Plantation Trace region. These landscapes are steeped in history and continue to support a robust agricultural community.

Iconic Islands and Wetlands

No discussion of Georgia's landscape would be complete without mentioning the barrier islands and the extensive wetlands. Places like Cumberland Island offer unspoiled natural beauty, historical sites, and unique ecosystems. The Okefenokee Swamp, one of the largest intact freshwater ecosystems in the world, provides critical habitat for a wide range of wildlife and offers visitors a glimpse into a vibrant, primordial landscape.

Rivers and Lakes

Georgia is also a state rich in rivers and lakes, which play a vital role in its ecosystem. The Savannah River, forming much of the border with South Carolina, flows through lush valleys and supports diverse plant and animal life. Lake Lanier, north of Atlanta, is a popular recreational spot that draws millions each year for boating, fishing, and water sports.

In Conclusion

Georgia's landscape is as varied as its history and culture. From the tidal marshes to mountain summits, from dynamic urban parks to tranquil waterways, the state's natural beauty offers something for every traveler. As you journey through these landscapes, remember that they are not just the backdrop but an integral part of Georgia's story.

The Flora and Fauna of Georgia

In *Georgia Travel Guide*, we journey beyond the cities and towns to explore the rich tapestry of natural life that Georgia harbors. This chapter is dedicated to exploring the diverse flora and fauna that enrich the landscapes of the Peach State, offering a glimpse into the vibrant ecosystems that thrive here.

Flora: A Botanical Mosaic

Georgia's flora is a vibrant mosaic, shaped by its varied geography—from the coastal plains to the rolling hills of central Georgia and the mountainous north. Each area boasts its own unique plant life.

Coastal Vegetation: Along the Atlantic coast, salt-tolerant grasses, sea oats, and saw palmettos dominate. The barrier islands, such as Cumberland Island, are known for their maritime forests, hosting diverse species including live oaks draped in Spanish moss.

Forests: Georgia is predominantly covered in lush deciduous and coniferous forests. Pines, oaks, and hickories are common, creating a dense canopy that is a haven for wildlife. The north Georgia mountains are home to higher altitude species like the Eastern hemlock and mountain laurel.

Wetlands and Marshes: Wetlands, such as those in the Okefenokee Swamp, are crucial for biodiversity. They support a variety of grasses, sedges, and the unique bald cypress. These areas are vital for water purification, flood control, and habitat for countless species.

Unique Species: Georgia is home to distinctive plant species like the Cherokee rose, the state flower, and the live oak, which is iconic in the southern landscapes. The state also protects several endangered plant species within its borders.

Fauna: From the Forests to the Seas

The animal life in Georgia is as diverse as its flora, ranging from marine species along the coastline to various mammals, birds, and insects in inland areas.

Marine Life: The coastal waters are bustling with life, including various species of whales, dolphins, and plentiful fish populations. The Georgia coast is a prime spot for observing loggerhead sea turtles, particularly during nesting and hatching season.

Birds: Georgia is a haven for birdwatchers. Coastal areas, such as the Altamaha Wildlife Management Area, attract migratory birds such as shorebirds and waterfowl. Inland, the forests and mountains are home to species like the red-tailed hawk, pileated woodpecker, and the state bird, the brown thrasher.

Mammals: The state's diverse habitats are inhabited by various mammals, including white-tailed deer, black bears, and bobcats. The elusive coyote can also be spotted across rural and even urban areas.

Insects and Reptiles: A variety of insects, including the vibrant eastern tiger swallowtail (the state butterfly), contribute to pollination and the ecological balance. Reptiles like the gopher tortoise, found in the state's sandy soils, are fascinating and play crucial roles in their ecosystems.

Preservation and Conservation Efforts

Georgia is committed to preserving its natural heritage. Various conservation programs and protected areas ensure the survival of many species and their habitats. Efforts like the Georgia Endangered Wildlife Program protect not only the well-known species but also the lesser known yet equally important plants and animals.

In Conclusion

The flora and fauna of Georgia are integral to the state's identity and allure. They add depth and color to the landscape and are essential for the ecological balance. As you explore the destinations in this guide, take a moment to appreciate the natural beauty and biodiversity that Georgia has to offer. It's not just about the places we visit, but also about the living tapestry that forms the backdrop of our journey.

The Climate of Georgia

In *Georgia Travel Guide*, the climate significantly shapes the experiences at each destination. This chapter delves into the climate of Georgia, providing insights into how it influences the landscapes, flora, fauna, and the overall travel experience throughout the state.

Seasonal Variations: A Year-Round Perspective

Georgia experiences a humid subtropical climate, marked by distinct seasonal changes that each bring their own unique charm and challenges.

Spring (March to May): This season sees a warming trend. Early spring might still be cool, but the state quickly bursts into color with blooming flowers such as azaleas and dogwoods. Spring rains are frequent, replenishing the natural landscapes and rivers.

Summer (June to August): Summers are typically hot and humid, with July and August experiencing the highest temperatures. Coastal areas benefit from ocean breezes, making beach destinations like Tybee Island and the Golden Isles especially popular. Inland areas, particularly in southern Georgia, can see temperatures soar.

Fall (September to November): Autumn brings cooler temperatures and less humidity, making it a perfect time for outdoor activities like hiking in the North Georgia Mountains. The foliage in these areas turns brilliant shades of red, orange, and yellow, attracting visitors for the spectacular display.

Winter (December to February): Winters are generally mild, with temperatures rarely dropping below freezing in the southern and coastal regions. However, the northern parts of the state, especially in the mountains, can experience light snowfall, creating beautiful winter landscapes ideal for cozy mountain retreats.

Regional Climate Differences

The climate in Georgia varies slightly from region to region:

Coastal Areas: These areas experience milder winters and cooler summers compared to the inland. Hurricanes or tropical storms can impact these regions, particularly from late summer to early fall.

Inland and Northern Altitudes: Regions away from the coast and in the higher altitudes of the North Georgia Mountains experience cooler temperatures overall and more significant seasonal changes. Winters can be chilly with occasional snowfall, and summers offer a pleasant escape from the heat of the lowlands.

Impact of Climate Change

Climate change is impacting Georgia, with rising temperatures and increasing humidity affecting the state. These changes impact the length and intensity of seasons and are being monitored for their long-term effects on the state's agriculture, natural environments, and tourism.

Preparing for Travel

When planning a visit to Georgia, consider the seasonal variations:

Spring and Summer: Pack light, breathable clothing for the day and something warmer for cooler evenings. Rain gear is also recommended due to frequent showers.

Fall: Layered clothing is ideal to adapt to the cool mornings and warmer afternoons.

Winter: Warm clothing is necessary for the northern mountain areas, including coats, hats, and gloves. Lighter layers may be sufficient in southern and coastal areas.

In Conclusion

The climate of Georgia adds to the state's appeal, providing a dynamic backdrop that changes with the seasons. Whether you're enjoying the vibrant spring blooms, cooling off at a beach in summer, admiring the fall foliage in the mountains, or exploring the historic towns in mild winter weather, understanding the climate will enhance your experience and help you prepare for a memorable visit.

The History of Georgia

In *Georgia Travel Guide*, the history of Georgia is not merely a backdrop but a fundamental component of the state's identity. This chapter takes you on a journey through time, exploring the rich historical tapestry that has shaped Georgia into the vibrant state it is today.

Indigenous Roots and Colonial Beginnings

Long before European settlers, Georgia was home to various Native American tribes, including the Creek and the Cherokee. Their presence and culture had a profound impact on the land.

The arrival of European settlers in the early 18th century marked the beginning of a new era. General James Oglethorpe established the colony of Georgia in 1733 in what is now Savannah. This period was marked by cooperation and conflict with native populations, shaping the early dynamics of the region.

A Crucial Role in the American Revolution

Georgia played a significant role in the American Revolution. It was one of the original Thirteen Colonies that rebelled against British rule in America. The Siege of Savannah in 1779 was one of the key battles during the Revolution, highlighting the strategic importance of Georgia in the fight for independence.

Antebellum Period and Civil War

The 19th century saw Georgia become heavily involved in the plantation economy and reliant on slavery, which led directly to its pivotal role in the Civil War. Georgia was one of the Confederate states, and the state saw significant battles such as the Battle of Atlanta and Sherman's infamous March to the Sea, which had lasting impacts on the state both physically and socially.

Reconstruction to Civil Rights

Post-Civil War, Georgia struggled through the Reconstruction era but later saw significant economic recovery. The 20th century marked a crucial period as Georgia became a major stage for the Civil Rights Movement. Leaders like Martin Luther King Jr. led nonviolent protests in Atlanta, shaping the fight for civil rights across the nation.

Modern Developments and Legacy

Throughout the 20th century and into the 21st, Georgia has remained at the forefront of social and economic change. It has become a hub for business, culture, and technology, with Atlanta often called the "Capital of the New South." The state has also been at the forefront of new social reforms and continues to play a significant role in national politics.

Historical Landmarks and Legacy

Georgia is dotted with historical landmarks. From the historic districts of Savannah, rich with antebellum architecture, to the Martin Luther King Jr. National Historical Park in Atlanta, and the battlegrounds of Chickamauga and Kennesaw Mountain, these sites offer a window into the past, allowing visitors to step back in time and experience the state's rich history.

In Conclusion

Understanding the history of Georgia is crucial to appreciating its present. From its indigenous roots to its crucial role in the birth of a nation, the ordeal of the Civil War, and its ongoing legacy of cultural and social progress, Georgia's history is a testament to the resilience and spirit of its people. As you explore the destinations in this guide, take a moment to reflect on the historical significance of each location, and how it has contributed to the tapestry that is Georgia today.

Atlanta and Surrounding Areas

1.   Mercedes-Benz Stadium, Atlanta

Mercedes-Benz Stadium stands as an icon of modern architecture and engineering in the heart of downtown Atlanta, Georgia. Officially opened in 2017, it serves as the home ground for the NFL's Atlanta Falcons and MLS's Atlanta United FC. Beyond its role as a sports venue, the stadium has quickly become a landmark for its state-of-the-art facilities and its commitment to sustainability.

The design of Mercedes-Benz Stadium is striking, featuring a unique pinwheel-shaped retractable roof and a façade of glass that allows natural light to flood the interior. The roof, which can open and close in just over seven minutes, consists of eight translucent panels that move along individual tracks, mimicking the aperture of a camera lens. This distinctive feature not only provides weather protection but also enhances the game-day experience with a dramatic, skyward view.

Inside, the stadium boasts one of the largest video boards in the world. The 360-degree halo board offers uninterrupted views of live action and replays, ensuring that every spectator has a superior visual experience from anywhere in the stands. With a capacity of over 71,000, which can expand to 75,000, the stadium offers a variety of seating options from general admission to premium luxury suites that cater to all levels of spectators.

Mercedes-Benz Stadium is renowned for its sustainable design, having achieved LEED Platinum certification, a first for a sports stadium in the United States. Features include highly efficient water systems, solar panels, and electric vehicle charging stations, which underline the venue's commitment to reducing its carbon footprint. The stadium's location was also strategically chosen for accessibility, encouraging the use of public transportation with its proximity to Atlanta's MARTA transit system.

2.   State Farm Arena, Atlanta

Located in the heart of downtown Atlanta, State Farm Arena is a premier venue for sports and entertainment, hosting over 160 events annually. Home to the NBA's Atlanta Hawks, the arena underwent a significant renovation in 2018, transforming it into a state-of-the-art facility focused on enhancing fan experience, accessibility, and sustainability.

The renovation of State Farm Arena was meticulously planned to create a more engaging and comfortable environment for spectators. The updates included the addition of new luxury suites, premium seating areas, and a variety of food and beverage options featuring local Atlanta cuisine. A unique aspect of the redesign is the "hawks bar," the first-ever courtside bar located within the seating area of an NBA arena.

With a seating capacity of approximately 17,000, the arena is designed to offer an intimate viewing experience, ensuring that every seat has an optimal view of the action. This design philosophy extends to concerts and other performances, making it one of Atlanta's most versatile venues. The arena also features a robust state-of-the-art sound system and a sophisticated lighting system that enhances both sports games and live performances.

State Farm Arena is not just a place for top-tier basketball and entertainment; it also plays a significant role in the community. The arena operates with a strong commitment to sustainability, incorporating practices like composting, recycling, and using energy-efficient systems to minimize its environmental impact. It has hosted various community events, including job fairs, educational programs, and health drives, reinforcing its role as a community hub.

The arena's downtown location places it within walking distance of other key Atlanta attractions, including the Mercedes-Benz Stadium and Centennial Olympic Park, making it a cornerstone in the city's vibrant entertainment district. Whether it's witnessing a thrilling basketball game or enjoying a live concert, State Farm Arena offers a dynamic and immersive experience for all visitors.

3.   College Football Hall of Fame, Atlanta

The College Football Hall of Fame in Atlanta is a must-visit for any sports enthusiast, especially those with a passion for college football. Relocated to Atlanta in 2014 from South Bend, Indiana, the facility is more than just a museum; it's an interactive experience that immerses visitors in the history and excitement of college football.

Spanning approximately 95,000 square feet, the Hall of Fame features a blend of historic college football artifacts and state-of-the-art interactive exhibits. Upon entering, visitors are greeted by a three-story wall of over 760 helmets, representing teams from around the country. This striking display sets the tone for a highly personalized experience, as guests can register their favorite team at the beginning of their visit and receive customized content as they move through the exhibits.

Interactive exhibits allow fans to engage in simulated games, listen to famous coaches' play calls, and even sing fight songs in a karaoke setup. The Hall of Fame's most cherished exhibit is the actual Hall of Fame, where visitors can learn about the players and coaches who have left a significant mark on college football through their skill, leadership, and sportsmanship.

The facility also includes a 45-yard indoor football field that hosts a variety of activities, allowing visitors to test their football skills. Throughout the year, the Hall of Fame offers educational programs and hosts special events, making it a vibrant part of Atlanta's cultural and educational landscape.

Located near other tourist attractions in downtown Atlanta, such as the Georgia Aquarium and the World of Coca-Cola, the College Football Hall of Fame is ideally situated for tourists looking to experience the rich sports culture of the South. It serves as a tribute to college football's legends and a source of inspiration and education for the next generation of fans and players.

4.   Centennial Olympic Park, Atlanta

Centennial Olympic Park, located in downtown Atlanta, is a sprawling public park that was originally built for the 1996 Summer Olympics. This 22-acre park remains a lasting legacy of the games and serves as a community gathering place and tourist destination, offering lush landscapes, interactive fountains, and expansive walkways.

One of the park's most famous features is the Fountain of Rings, an interactive fountain that incorporates the Olympic Ring symbol. This fountain offers both a visually appealing water show and a place for children to cool off during the hot Atlanta summers. The park also features several sculptures and artworks that celebrate the spirit of the Olympics and the diverse cultural contributions of the games.

Centennial Olympic Park is not just a place for relaxation and recreation; it also serves as a venue for major concerts, festivals, and seasonal events. The park's expansive lawns and performance pavilion make it an ideal location for large-scale events in the heart of the city. Events like Fourth of July celebrations, music festivals, and food festivals are regular occurrences, drawing both locals and tourists alike.

In addition to its role as an event space, the park has spurred significant development in the surrounding area, including the construction of new attractions, hotels, and commercial spaces. Its proximity to other major attractions like the Georgia Aquarium, the World of Coca-Cola, and the State Farm Arena makes it a central component of Atlanta's tourist circuit.

Centennial Olympic Park also offers quiet spots for reflection, with lush gardens and panoramic views of the Atlanta skyline. It is a place where visitors can enjoy the beauty and vibrancy of Atlanta while remembering the historic events of the 1996 Olympics that showcased the city to the world.

5.   World of Coca-Cola, Atlanta

The World of Coca-Cola in Atlanta, Georgia, is more than just a museum; it is an immersive experience into the world of the most iconic soft drink brand on the planet. Spanning approximately 92,000 square feet, the World of Coca-Cola offers a variety of interactive exhibits, historical artifacts, and multimedia presentations that detail the fascinating story of Coca-Cola's inception in 1886 by Dr. John S. Pemberton, to its current status as a global phenomenon. Upon entering, visitors are greeted by an impressive lobby featuring a Coca-Cola bottle chandelier and a variety of memorabilia that sets the stage for the journey ahead.

One of the main attractions is the 'Vault of the Secret Formula', where guests can learn about the secretive and heavily guarded recipe of Coca-Cola. This exhibit delves into the myths and lore surrounding one of the best-kept secrets in the food and beverage industry. Another highlight is 'Milestones of Refreshment', a timeline exhibit that showcases vintage bottles, advertisements, and other memorabilia that trace the evolution of the brand through the decades.

A fan favorite is the 'Taste It!' exhibit, where visitors can sample over 100 different Coca-Cola beverages from around the world. From the popular familiar flavors to the exotic and unusual, this tasting experience is often a highlight of the visit.

The World of Coca-Cola also offers a 4-D theater experience featuring a multi-sensory movie that takes visitors on a fantastical journey involving the secret formula. Additionally, the venue hosts a fully functional bottling line that gives visitors a firsthand look at the bottling process, from start to finish, providing insight into the complexity and scale of Coca-Cola's manufacturing processes.

The venue is not just about history and tasting; it's a place where art meets branding. The Pop Culture Gallery displays artworks inspired by Coca-Cola by various artists, illustrating the significant impact that this brand has had on popular culture and the arts over the years.

For those looking to take a piece of Coke history home, the Coca-Cola Store offers a wide range of merchandise from apparel to unique art pieces, making it the perfect ending to the tour.

6. Georgia Aquarium, Atlanta

The Georgia Aquarium, located in downtown Atlanta near other major attractions like the World of Coca-Cola and Centennial Olympic Park, is one of the largest aquariums in the world and an engineering marvel that provides habitat for thousands of animals, representing several hundred species, all contained in more than 10 million gallons of fresh and saltwater. Since its opening in 2005, it has been a premier destination for marine life education and conservation.

Visitors to the Georgia Aquarium can explore different global aquatic environments through the facility's beautifully designed galleries. Each exhibit is designed to provide an immersive experience that mimics the natural habitats of the species it houses. The Ocean Voyager exhibit, for instance, features a 100-foot-long underwater tunnel and one of the largest single aquatic exhibits in the world. This exhibit alone is home to thousands of fish including the gentle giants of the sea, whale sharks, and manta rays.

The Cold Water Quest gallery showcases animals from the colder reaches of the ocean, like beluga whales, African penguins, and sea otters, while the Tropical Diver exhibit dazzles with bright coral reefs and an array of tropical fish. A particularly engaging experience is the aquarium's interactive touch pools, where visitors can touch various marine animals under the guidance of trained staff, enhancing the hands-on learning experience.

The Georgia Aquarium is also heavily involved in research and conservation efforts. It operates numerous research initiatives aimed at marine life conservation, veterinary care, and environmental protection. The aquarium's commitment to education is evident in its numerous educational programs and interactive shows that aim to inspire guests to appreciate marine life and understand the importance of ocean conservation.

For those looking for a more in-depth exploration, the aquarium offers behind-the-scenes tours where guests can learn about the care of marine animals and the operations that support the running of such a massive facility. The aquarium also offers unique animal encounter programs that allow guests to swim or dive with certain species, providing an up-close and personal experience that is both educational and thrilling.

7.   Fox Theatre, Atlanta

The Fox Theatre, located in Midtown Atlanta, is one of the city's premier venues for live entertainment. Opened in 1929, originally as a movie palace, the Fox Theatre's unique blend of Egyptian and Spanish architectural styles makes it one of the most iconic landmarks in Atlanta. Its elaborate design and grandiose interior, which includes a ceiling designed to resemble a starlit sky, make every visit a memorable experience.

The theatre was originally developed by the Shriners organization but was opened to the public to recoup the costs incurred during its construction. Throughout its history, the Fox Theatre has faced numerous challenges, including financial difficulties and a demolition threat in the 1970s, which led to a massive public campaign to save it. Today, it stands not only as a functioning theatre but also as a historical monument to the community's resilience and commitment to preserving cultural heritage.

The Fox Theatre hosts a wide range of performances, from Broadway shows and live concerts to comedy shows and classic movie screenings. Its 4,665-seat auditorium, with its excellent acoustics and intimate seating arrangement, ensures that every event is a special experience. The venue's majestic atmosphere and historical significance enhance the appeal of the performances it hosts.

In addition to its main auditorium, the Fox Theatre features the Egyptian Ballroom and the Grand Salon, which are used for private events such as weddings, galas, and corporate gatherings. These spaces, adorned with elaborate decorations and historic motifs, offer a unique and elegant setting for special events.

The Fox Theatre is not only a hub of entertainment but also a vital part of Atlanta's cultural scene, offering educational programs and tours that highlight its architectural beauty and historical importance. These tours provide insights into the theatre's past, its architectural details, and the legends that have graced its stage, making it a must-visit for anyone interested in the arts, architecture, or history.

8.   High Museum of Art, Atlanta

Located in the heart of Atlanta's arts district, the High Museum of Art is the leading art museum in the Southeastern United States, housing a diverse and expansive collection of more than 15,000 works. Its impressive assortment includes classic to contemporary art, with significant holdings of European paintings, African American art, and modern and contemporary pieces.

The High Museum's striking building, designed by renowned architect Richard Meier and later expanded by Renzo Piano, is a work of art in itself. Its bright, airy spaces and innovative design elements provide a perfect backdrop for the art within and make the museum a visual landmark in Atlanta.

The museum's permanent collection includes works by many of the greatest artists from around the world, including Claude Monet, Martin Johnson Heade, and Giovanni Battista Tiepolo, along with modern masters such as Chuck Close and Gerhard Richter. The collection is particularly noted for its extensive anthology of 19th and 20th-century American art and a growing collection of contemporary art that includes works by many pivotal African American artists.

In addition to its permanent holdings, the High Museum of Art hosts several high-profile traveling exhibitions each year, which have included shows ranging from Renaissance art to modern photography and everything in between. These exhibitions serve to enhance the museum's offerings and provide visitors with a dynamic and ever-changing viewing experience.

Educational outreach is a core part of the High Museum's mission. It offers an array of educational programs and community outreach initiatives designed to engage audiences of all ages. From lectures and workshops to family days and school programs, the museum seeks to educate and inspire visitors through direct engagement with art.

As a cultural hub, the High Museum of Art plays a pivotal role in Atlanta's arts community, offering a space for exploration and appreciation of the arts that is accessible to all. Its commitment to excellence in collecting, conserving, and educating makes it a premier destination for art lovers and a vital institution for cultural enrichment in the region.

9.   Atlanta Botanical Garden, Atlanta

The Atlanta Botanical Garden offers a lush paradise spread over 30 acres that features an impressive collection of plants from around the world. This urban oasis is dedicated to the study and conservation of plants, providing both a refuge for enjoyment and an educational resource that promotes understanding of botanical science.

Upon entering the Atlanta Botanical Garden, visitors are greeted by a variety of thematic gardens and plant collections that showcase different habitats and botanical themes. The Garden includes the Dorothy Chapman Fuqua Conservatory, which houses tropical rainforest and desert plants, and offers a chance to see rare and endangered species from across the globe.

One of the most breathtaking features of the garden is the Canopy Walk, a 600-foot-long skywalk that allows visitors to tour one of the city's last remaining urban forests from 40 feet in the air. This unique perspective gives a bird's eye view of the woodland garden below, emphasizing the beauty and importance of preserving natural landscapes.

The Garden also hosts the Earth Goddess, a massive living sculpture that is part of the "Imaginary Worlds" exhibit. This and other fantastical plant sculptures throughout the garden are examples of mosaiculture, a horticultural art that involves creating giant topiary-like structures covered in plants.

The Atlanta Botanical Garden is not only a place to wander and admire the beauty of nature but also a center for education and cultural events. It offers a range of classes and workshops for all ages, covering topics such as gardening, photography, and botanical illustration. Additionally, the Garden hosts various seasonal events, including the popular Garden Lights, Holiday Nights, which features spectacular light displays throughout the garden during the holiday season.

The commitment of the Atlanta Botanical Garden to conservation is evident through its various research initiatives and conservation programs. The Garden actively participates in global conservation, focusing on rare and endangered species in Georgia and around the world. It's a place where beauty and science converge, offering visitors not only the chance to enjoy nature but to learn about its delicate balance and the importance of preserving our natural world.

10.   Piedmont Park, Atlanta

Piedmont Park is Atlanta's most iconic green space and a central gathering place for the community. Spanning over 200 acres in the heart of Midtown, the park offers a plethora of activities and amenities, including walking and jogging paths, playgrounds, tennis courts, and the picturesque Lake Clara Meer. Its expansive lawns and panoramic views of the Atlanta skyline make it a popular location for outdoor concerts, festivals, and a variety of cultural events.

Originally designed by the sons of Frederick Law Olmsted, who designed New York's Central Park, Piedmont Park has grown through several phases of expansion and renovation to become the city's premier urban park. It blends historic charm with modern amenities, offering something for everyone. Whether it's participating in organized sports, enjoying a leisurely picnic, or attending one of the many annual events like the Atlanta Dogwood Festival and the Atlanta Jazz Festival, the park serves as Atlanta's "common ground."

Piedmont Park is also home to the Atlanta Botanical Garden, adding a dimension of botanical beauty and educational value to the park's landscape. The active and vibrant atmosphere of Piedmont Park is complemented by its role as a serene escape where people can relax beside the lake or stroll through the quiet walking trails that crisscross the park.

Environmental sustainability is a key focus for Piedmont Park, which features extensive biking paths and green initiatives. The park has been a leader in conservation efforts within the city, featuring extensive rain gardens and energy-efficient facilities. Its community garden, open to local residents, promotes sustainable urban agriculture and provides a space for growing vegetables and herbs in the heart of the city.

For residents and visitors alike, Piedmont Park represents the social and cultural heart of Atlanta. Its vast open spaces not only offer recreation and relaxation but also serve as a venue for major public events and private gatherings, reflecting the dynamic spirit of Atlanta.

11.   Ponce City Market, Atlanta

Ponce City Market is one of Atlanta's most vibrant and popular destinations, situated in the historic Sears, Roebuck & Co. building in the Old Fourth Ward. This mixed-use development seamlessly combines retail, residential, and office spaces, making it a hub of activity day and night. Its central location on the Atlanta BeltLine connects it to various parts of the city, enhancing its accessibility and appeal.

The transformation of the massive historic structure into Ponce City Market is a key example of successful urban revitalization. The market features a central food hall that offers a range of dining options from some of Atlanta's top chefs and restaurateurs. From quick bites to gourmet meals, the food hall is a culinary destination that reflects the diversity of Atlanta's food scene.

Beyond its culinary offerings, Ponce City Market includes a broad array of shops ranging from local artisan boutiques to international brands, making it a prime location for shopping in the city. The upper floors of the building are home to residential lofts and modern office spaces, which contribute to the dynamic and urban atmosphere of the market.

One of the most distinctive features of Ponce City Market is The Roof, offering recreational activities, including a mini-golf course, amusement park rides, and an extensive beer garden with panoramic views of the city. This rooftop area provides a unique space for leisure and socializing, further establishing Ponce City Market as a multi-faceted destination.

Ponce City Market not only serves as a center for eating, shopping, and living but also engages with the community through events and activities that take place throughout the year. These include seasonal events, live music performances, and educational workshops, which are integral to its role as a community hub.

12.   Fernbank Museum of Natural History, Atlanta

Fernbank Museum of Natural History, located near Emory University in Atlanta, is an exceptional venue dedicated to exploring the natural world. Through a combination of static and interactive exhibits, large-format films, and educational programs, the museum offers visitors insights into the dynamic processes and forces that have shaped the earth and its ecosystems.

One of the museum's most striking features is its Great Hall, which houses the "Giants of the Mesozoic" exhibit. This display features a full-scale replica of the Argentinosaurus, one of the largest dinosaurs ever discovered, alongside a Giganotosaurus, creating a dramatic depiction of life during the Mesozoic era. This exhibit, along with others in the museum's extensive permanent collection, helps illustrate the diversity and history of life on Earth, from the prehistoric to the present.

The museum is also home to the Fernbank Forest, a 65-acre old-growth forest that offers visitors a rare chance to experience a pristine hardwood forest ecosystem in the heart of metropolitan Atlanta. Guided tours and educational walks through the forest are available, providing insights into the native flora and fauna and the ecological processes that sustain them.

Fernbank's 3D IMAX theater presents a range of films that explore various aspects of science, nature, and culture. These films are designed to educate and inspire audiences about the natural world and human civilization in an immersive setting.

Beyond its exhibits and films, Fernbank Museum of Natural History is actively involved in scientific research and educational outreach. It hosts a variety of programs aimed at students and educators, designed to enhance science literacy and encourage conservation. Seasonal events, adult-themed evenings, and family activities are also part of the museum's offerings, making it a versatile destination for learners of all ages.

13.　Martin Luther King Jr. National Historic Site, Atlanta

The Martin Luther King Jr. National Historic Site in Atlanta, Georgia, stands as a profound testament to the life and legacy of one of America's most influential civil rights leaders. Spanning several city blocks in the Sweet Auburn neighborhood, the site encompasses the birthplace, church, and final resting place of Dr. Martin Luther King Jr., offering visitors a deeply moving insight into his life, work, and the times in which he lived.

Visitors to the site are first welcomed at the Visitor Center, which features exhibits that chronicle Dr. King's life and the progress of the American Civil Rights Movement. Through interactive displays, personal artifacts, and multimedia presentations, these exhibits provide a contextual background that enhances the understanding of King's development as a leader and his enduring impact on world history.

One of the most significant components of the historic site is Dr. King's boyhood home on Auburn Avenue. Restored to its 1930s appearance, the home is available to the public through guided tours, which are led by National Park Service rangers. These tours offer a glimpse into the early life of Dr. King, highlighting the familial and community influences that shaped his philosophies and leadership.

Just a short walk from his childhood home is Ebenezer Baptist Church, where both Dr. King and his father served as pastors. Here, visitors can sit in the pews, listen to his sermons play over the speakers, and reflect on the profound messages that galvanized the movement for equality and justice. The church remains a cornerstone of the community and a vivid symbol of Dr. King's commitment to nonviolent protest.

Across from the church is The King Center, established by Coretta Scott King in 1968. The center includes Dr. King's final resting place, a peaceful reflecting pool, and the Eternal Flame symbolizing the ongoing fight for justice and peace. The King Center also contains the Freedom Hall, which hosts exhibitions on Dr. King, Mrs. King, and other leaders of the civil rights and global peace movements.

14. Zoo Atlanta, Atlanta

Zoo Atlanta, located in historic Grant Park, is one of Georgia's most loved family attractions. Established in 1889, the zoo has grown from a small menagerie into a premier zoological institution known for its leadership in conservation, education, and animal care. Zoo Atlanta houses over 1,000 animals representing more than 200 species from around the world, including one of the nation's largest collections of gorillas and orangutans.

The zoo is renowned for its innovative exhibits, such as the Ford African Rain Forest, which has played a vital role in the conservation and breeding of western lowland gorillas. Visitors can observe these magnificent creatures in a habitat that mimics their natural environment, providing an up-close look at their complex social interactions and behaviors.

Another highlight is the Giant Panda Conservation Center, home to the zoo's beloved giant pandas. Zoo Atlanta is one of only a few zoos in the U.S. to house these rare animals and has been remarkably successful in their breeding program. The pandas are a favorite among visitors, who can watch them play, eat, and interact with their environment.

Beyond viewing exotic animals, visitors to Zoo Atlanta can participate in a variety of educational programs and experiences designed to foster an appreciation for wildlife and the natural world. These include Keeper Talks, behind-the-scenes tours, and interactive wildlife shows. For younger visitors, the zoo offers the Treetop Trail, a ropes course that allows children to navigate through the trees just as some of their favorite animals might.

Zoo Atlanta is deeply committed to conservation, supporting over 40 conservation projects both locally and internationally. By visiting the zoo, guests contribute to these efforts, helping to fund wildlife research and habitat preservation initiatives that benefit species at the zoo and in the wild.

Zoo Atlanta provides an enjoyable and enlightening experience for all ages, combining fun with education and conservation. It remains a must-visit Atlanta attraction for anyone interested in animals, nature, and conservation.

15.   Six Flags Over Georgia, Austell

Six Flags Over Georgia, located just outside Atlanta in Austell, is the largest regional theme park in the Southeast. Since its opening in 1967, it has been a major destination for thrill-seekers and families alike, offering a wide array of rides, shows, and attractions spread across 290 acres.

The park features over 40 rides, including 11 roller coasters and numerous family-friendly attractions. Thrill-seekers flock to rides like Goliath and Twisted Cyclone for their high speeds and intense loops, while families enjoy gentler options such as the Hanson Cars or the historic Riverview Carousel, one of the largest carousels in the world.

Six Flags Over Georgia is also known for its themed areas that capture the culture and history of the regions they represent. From the charm of the Georgia section to the spooky vibes of Gotham City, each area offers a unique atmosphere and themed rides that enhance the visitor experience. The park's seasonal events, like Fright Fest and Holiday in the Park, provide additional entertainment with themed decorations, performances, and activities that change throughout the year.

In addition to rides and entertainment, Six Flags Over Georgia offers a variety of dining options and shopping outlets. From classic amusement park snacks like funnel cakes and cotton candy to sit-down dining experiences, there's something to satisfy every appetite.

As a leader in entertainment, Six Flags Over Georgia not only provides fun and excitement but also focuses on safety and guest services, ensuring that each visit is enjoyable and secure. With its ever-evolving array of rides and attractions, Six Flags Over Georgia remains a staple of family entertainment in the Atlanta area, drawing visitors from all over the region and beyond.

16.   Silver Comet Trail, Smyrna

The Silver Comet Trail is a free-access pathway that stretches for 61.5 miles from Smyrna, Georgia, to the Georgia-Alabama state line, where it connects with the Chief Ladiga Trail. This scenic trail is built on the abandoned railway line once used by the Silver Comet passenger train, and it offers a serene and picturesque route for walkers, cyclists, and horseback riders.

The trail is renowned for its accessibility and beauty, providing a linear oasis away from the hustle and bustle of urban Atlanta. As it winds through small towns, lush forests, and over trestles, the Silver Comet Trail offers diverse scenery that changes with the seasons. The flat, paved path is ideal for all ages and abilities, making it a popular destination for families, casual hikers, serious cyclists, and outdoor enthusiasts.

Along the route, there are numerous access points, parking areas, restrooms, and picnic areas, making it convenient for visitors to plan their trip according to their needs. The trail is also equipped with mile markers and informational signs that provide historical context and highlight the natural features of the surrounding landscape.

One of the most spectacular features along the Silver Comet Trail is the Pumpkinvine Creek Trestle, which stands over 750 feet long and 100 feet high, offering expansive views of the creek and surrounding forest. This and other trestles along the route offer not only stunning vistas but also a unique perspective on the natural beauty of the area.

The Silver Comet Trail is more than just a recreational path; it's a community resource that provides a safe and beautiful environment for physical activity, relaxation, and communion with nature. Its contribution to the health and well-being of the community is immeasurable, as it encourages outdoor activity and provides a venue for community events and races.

Whether looking for a leisurely stroll, a vigorous bike ride, or a scenic horseback ride, the Silver Comet Trail offers a perfect setting. Its combination of natural beauty, historical significance, and excellent amenities make it one of Georgia's premier outdoor destinations.

17.   Atlanta History Center, Atlanta

The Atlanta History Center is a comprehensive educational facility dedicated to exploring and understanding the rich and diverse history of Atlanta and the Southeastern United States.

A standout feature of the Atlanta History Center is the Swan House, an elegantly restored 1928 mansion that epitomizes the prosperity and glamour of Atlanta in the early 20th century. The house is often used as a filming location and is beloved for its classical architecture and beautifully maintained gardens. Another historic landmark on the grounds is the Smith Family Farm, which provides insights into Georgia's rural heritage with its original farmhouse, slave cabins, barn, and smithy, all surrounded by reconstructed gardens and farmyard.

In addition to these historic houses, the Center is home to the Atlanta History Museum, which houses one of the Southeast's largest history collections. Permanent and temporary exhibitions offer a deep dive into various aspects of local and national history, including Native American cultures, the Civil War, the Civil Rights Movement, and the 1996 Atlanta Olympics. The museum's interactive exhibits, such as a full-scale locomotive and a replica of a historic tavern, are particularly engaging for visitors of all ages.

The Kenan Research Center is another integral part of the Atlanta History Center. This archive offers an extensive array of primary sources, including maps, books, manuscripts, and photographs, which are invaluable resources for researchers and history enthusiasts.

The Center also features the Goizueta Gardens, which include nine distinct landscapes that showcase the horticultural history of the Southeast. These gardens range from a formal garden at the Swan House to a woodland trail filled with native plants, providing a tranquil retreat and a learning environment about local flora and sustainable gardening practices.

Throughout the year, the Atlanta History Center hosts a variety of events and educational programs that cater to diverse interests, including author lectures, history camps for children, and seasonal festivals. These programs further the Center's mission to connect people, history, and culture.

18.   The Battery Atlanta and Truist Park, Atlanta

The Battery Atlanta, located just northwest of downtown Atlanta, is a modern mixed-use development that encapsulates the vibrancy of urban life. Anchored by Truist Park, the home of the Atlanta Braves Major League Baseball team, this destination combines entertainment, shopping, dining, and residential living into one dynamic environment.

Truist Park, with a seating capacity of over 41,000, provides a fan-first experience with closer seats for better views, open concourses, and modern amenities that ensure every game is memorable. The park's design reflects the charm of classic ballparks while integrating state-of-the-art technology to enhance the game day atmosphere. It's not just about baseball; Truist Park hosts concerts, festivals, and other community events, making it a year-round entertainment hub.

Surrounding the ballpark, The Battery Atlanta offers an array of experiences. With over 1.5 million square feet of retail space, it features a blend of premier shopping, dining, and entertainment venues. Restaurants range from casual eateries to fine dining, featuring local and international cuisines. The retail spaces include boutique shops, major brands, and everything in between, catering to a broad spectrum of styles and preferences.

For entertainment, The Battery Atlanta includes venues like the Coca-Cola Roxy Theatre, which hosts concerts and private events, and a variety of bars and clubs that offer live music and nightlife. The development also includes a multi-use theater, bowling alley, and an escape room experience, providing fun and entertainment for all ages.

Living options at The Battery Atlanta include luxury apartments and condos that offer residents a lively urban lifestyle with the convenience of amenities and attractions right on their doorstep. The integration of work, live, and play elements within The Battery Atlanta reflects a growing trend in urban planning aimed at creating vibrant, sustainable communities.

19. Kennesaw Mountain National Battlefield Park, Kennesaw

Kennesaw Mountain National Battlefield Park, located in Kennesaw, Georgia, is a 2,965-acre park preserving the site of a significant Civil War battle. In June 1864, the Battle of Kennesaw Mountain was fought here as part of the Atlanta Campaign, and today, the park serves as a tribute to those who fought and an educational resource on the Civil War.

Visitors to Kennesaw Mountain National Battlefield Park can explore a network of historical and interpretive trails that provide insights into the strategies and experiences of both Union and Confederate forces. The park's visitor center offers exhibits on the battle and the broader context of the Civil War in Georgia, including artifacts, uniforms, and weaponry.

One of the most popular activities in the park is hiking to the summit of Kennesaw Mountain. The hike is not only a physical challenge but also provides panoramic views of the Atlanta skyline and the North Georgia mountains. Along the way, interpretive signs detail the significance of various locations within the park, including fortifications, battlegrounds, and historic farmsteads.

The park is also a significant habitat for wildlife and native plants, with extensive meadows, forests, and wetlands that have reclaimed the landscape over the decades. Bird watching is particularly rewarding here, with the park being a popular site for migratory and resident birds.

Educational programs at Kennesaw Mountain National Battlefield Park are designed to enhance visitors' understanding of the historical and natural significance of the site. These programs include guided tours, living history demonstrations, and special events on Memorial Day and Veterans Day, emphasizing the park's role in commemorating military history.

The park's preservation efforts ensure that Kennesaw Mountain National Battlefield Park remains a valuable educational and recreational resource, offering a blend of history, nature, and recreation that appeals to visitors of all ages and interests.

20.   Chattahoochee Nature Center, Roswell

Located in Roswell, Georgia, just north of Atlanta, the Chattahoochee Nature Center is a private non-profit that sits on 127 acres along the Chattahoochee River. Established in 1976, the center is dedicated to educating visitors about the ecology of the Chattahoochee River and its watershed, promoting conservation and environmental stewardship through its interactive exhibits, wildlife programs, and conservation efforts.

The center includes a variety of habitats, including wetlands, forests, and river ecosystems, which are home to a wide range of wildlife. Visitors can explore these habitats via a network of trails and boardwalks that provide up-close views of plants and animals native to the Georgia Piedmont region. The Discovery Center, an interpretive building at the heart of the nature center, features hands-on exhibits that explore the area's natural history and the importance of preserving natural habitats.

One of the key attractions of the Chattahoochee Nature Center is its wildlife rehabilitation program. The center operates a clinic that cares for injured and orphaned wildlife with the goal of returning them to the wild. Visitors can learn about the rehabilitation process and see some of the current patients through viewing windows, gaining insight into the challenges these animals face.

The center also offers a range of educational programs for all ages, including guided hikes, canoe trips on the Chattahoochee River, and interactive classes about the environment and wildlife. These programs are designed to foster a connection with nature and inspire the next generation of environmental stewards.

Seasonal events at the Chattahoochee Nature Center, such as the Butterfly Festival and Halloween Hikes, provide additional opportunities for community engagement and education, making the center a vital part of the local community and a leader in environmental education in the Atlanta area.

21.   North Point Mall, Alpharetta

North Point Mall, located in the vibrant city of Alpharetta, Georgia, is a premier shopping destination that offers a wide range of retail, dining, and entertainment options. Since its opening in 1993, the mall has been a key attraction for both locals and visitors, providing a spacious and modern environment for shopping enthusiasts.

Spanning over 1.3 million square feet, North Point Mall is home to more than 100 stores, featuring a mix of high-end and mainstream retail brands. Anchored by major department stores such as Macy's, Dillard's, and JCPenney, the mall also boasts a selection of specialty shops that cater to a diverse array of tastes and preferences. From fashion and beauty to electronics and home decor, the mall's comprehensive retail offerings ensure a satisfying shopping experience for all ages.

The mall is not just about shopping; it includes a variety of dining options that range from casual eats to fine dining. The food court and surrounding eateries offer a plethora of culinary choices, accommodating those looking for a quick bite as well as visitors wanting a more relaxed meal. In addition, North Point Mall features several full-service restaurants where shoppers can unwind and enjoy a variety of dishes.

For entertainment, North Point Mall houses a state-of-the-art AMC Theatre that provides a perfect escape for movie-goers to enjoy the latest blockbusters. The mall also hosts regular events that include seasonal festivities, live music performances, and family-friendly activities, making it a community hub full of vibrancy and engagement.

The architecture of North Point Mall is designed for convenience, with an inviting atmosphere that includes wide, well-lit corridors and comfortable seating areas. Accessibility is a priority, ensuring that all facilities are easily navigable for families with strollers and individuals with disabilities.

Overall, North Point Mall stands out as a comprehensive shopping and entertainment complex. It continues to attract visitors with its blend of retail variety, dining options, and entertainment activities, all set within a friendly and welcoming environment.

22. Avalon, Alpharetta

Avalon is an upscale, mixed-use development in Alpharetta, Georgia, that seamlessly blends shopping, dining, residential, and office components into a cohesive community experience. Since its opening in 2014, Avalon has set a new standard for a luxury lifestyle and retail destination.

Spanning over 86 acres, Avalon features more than 500,000 square feet of retail space with over 130 premium stores and boutiques. These include flagship locations from major brands as well as local retailers that offer exclusive products. The shopping experience at Avalon is enhanced by its focus on luxury and quality, appealing to discerning shoppers looking for high-end merchandise.

The dining scene at Avalon is equally impressive, with more than 20 restaurants and eateries that provide a range of culinary experiences from quick casual to gourmet dining. The development is known for attracting top chefs and unique dining concepts, offering dishes that cater to every palate and occasion.

Avalon is not just a place to shop and dine; it is a vibrant community hub. The development includes luxury rental residences and single-family homes, making it a truly integrated live-work-play environment. The office spaces at Avalon attract businesses looking for a dynamic and engaging community atmosphere.

Community events are central to Avalon's appeal. The development hosts a wide array of events throughout the year, including seasonal festivals, live concerts, outdoor movie nights, and markets that showcase local artisans and producers. These events, coupled with Avalon's elegant central plaza, water features, and green spaces, create a lively public space that encourages community interaction and enjoyment.

For families, Avalon offers several amenities and activities, including a seasonal ice-skating rink, a children's play area, and interactive fountains that are popular during the summer months. Security and concierge services ensure a safe and comfortable environment, enhancing the overall experience for all visitors.

23.　Lake Lanier Islands, Buford

Lake Lanier Islands is a resort complex located on Lake Lanier in Buford, Georgia, renowned for its scenic beauty and a wide range of recreational activities. Spanning several thousand acres, the islands offer a perfect getaway with water parks, golf courses, boating, and a host of other entertainment options, making it a popular destination for families, couples, and solo travelers alike.

The centerpiece of Lake Lanier Islands is Margaritaville at Lanier Islands, a comprehensive water park that features a variety of water attractions, including wave pools, slides, and an adventure course. The water park is themed around the laid-back, tropical vibe of Jimmy Buffett's famous song, offering a fun and relaxing beach experience with white sands and clear waters.

For boating enthusiasts, Lake Lanier is a prime destination. Visitors can rent boats, jet skis, or kayaks to explore the expansive lake, which stretches over 38,000 acres. Fishing is another popular activity, with the lake well-stocked with bass, catfish, and trout. Guided fishing tours and tournaments are regularly held, attracting anglers of all skill levels.

The resort also includes a championship golf course, Lanier Islands Legacy Golf Course, known for its challenging layout and stunning lake views. The course provides a rewarding experience for golfers, with well-maintained fairways and greens and a full-service clubhouse.

Accommodation options at Lake Lanier Islands range from luxury suites at the Legacy Lodge, which offers comfortable, refined lodging with lake views, to lakeside villas and campgrounds that provide a more intimate connection with the natural surroundings. The variety of accommodations ensures that all guests can find something to suit their tastes and budgets.

Lake Lanier Islands also hosts a variety of events and festivals throughout the year, including elaborate holiday light displays during the winter season, which transform the islands into a magical winter wonderland. Summer concerts, wine tastings, and culinary events further enhance the appeal of Lake Lanier Islands as a year-round destination.

24. Mall of Georgia, Buford

Located in Buford, the Mall of Georgia is the largest shopping mall in the state and one of the key retail destinations in the Southeast. With over 200 stores, a 20-screen movie theater, and numerous dining and entertainment options, the mall is a dynamic center for shopping, socializing, and entertainment.

The Mall of Georgia features a wide array of retailers from high-end fashion brands to popular chain stores, ensuring a comprehensive shopping experience that caters to a variety of tastes and budgets. Major anchor stores like Macy's, Nordstrom, Dillard's, and JCPenney are complemented by a diverse selection of specialty shops that offer everything from clothing and accessories to home goods and technology.

In addition to shopping, the mall boasts a range of dining options, from fast food to fine dining. The food court offers quick bites while standalone restaurants around the mall provide sit-down meals, catering to shoppers looking for a break or a place to meet up with friends and family.

The Mall of Georgia is not just about retail and food; it also provides a variety of entertainment options. The Regal Cinemas complex includes an IMAX theater, offering the latest movies in a state-of-the-art viewing environment. The mall's outdoor village area hosts concerts and family-friendly events throughout the year, including a summer concert series and holiday celebrations, adding to the vibrant atmosphere of the mall.

For families, the Mall of Georgia offers several amenities, including a children's play area and interactive fountains that are perfect for cooling off in the summer. The spacious layout and ample seating areas throughout the mall make it a comfortable place for visitors to relax and enjoy their day.

Overall, the Mall of Georgia is more than just a shopping destination; it is a bustling hub of activity where shopping, dining, and entertainment converge to offer a fulfilling visit for locals and tourists alike.

25.   Stone Mountain Park, Stone Mountain

Stone Mountain Park, located just outside Atlanta in Stone Mountain, Georgia, is a vast, 3,200-acre park that is centered around the world's largest piece of exposed granite, Stone Mountain. The park is one of Georgia's most popular attractions, offering a wide range of activities for all ages and interests, including historical exhibits, natural beauty, and recreational activities.

Visitors to Stone Mountain Park can explore a variety of attractions. The Summit Skyride, a high-speed Swiss cable car, provides a scenic ride to the top of Stone Mountain, offering expansive views of the Atlanta skyline and the Appalachian Mountains. At the top, visitors can walk around, enjoy the panoramic vistas, and inspect the Confederate Memorial Carving, which depicts three Confederate leaders of the Civil War.

The park also offers a rich history that is explored through attractions like the Antebellum Plantation and Farmyard, which is a collection of original buildings that have been restored to reflect the pre-Civil War era. This living history museum offers insight into 18th and 19th-century Southern life, with costumed interpreters demonstrating period crafts and farming techniques.

For outdoor enthusiasts, Stone Mountain Park features more than 15 miles of hiking and walking trails, including the popular Walk-Up Trail that leads to the summit of the mountain. The park's lakes offer fishing, kayaking, and canoeing opportunities, while its vast green spaces are perfect for picnicking and kite flying.

Family entertainment is plentiful at Stone Mountain Park with seasonal events like the Pumpkin Festival, Spring FUN Break, and the spectacular Stone Mountain Christmas celebration, which features live shows, parades, and fireworks. One of the highlights is the Lasershow Spectacular, projected onto the side of Stone Mountain, which combines music, light effects, and fireworks to celebrate the spirit of Atlanta.

Coastal and Southern Georgia

1. Savannah Historic District, Savannah

The Savannah Historic District, a National Historic Landmark, is the heart of one of the most beautiful cities in Georgia and arguably the United States. Known for its cobblestone streets, lush green squares, and well-preserved Antebellum architecture, this area offers a picturesque window into the past, capturing the essence of Southern charm and history.

Covering approximately 2.5 square miles, the Historic District is a living museum of American architecture from the colonial 18th century through the Victorian period of the 19th century. It was one of the first cities in Georgia to be planned around a system of squares, and today 22 of these squares still exist, providing peaceful green spaces amid the urban landscape. Each square is surrounded by stunning examples of Georgian, Gothic, and Greek Revival buildings that have been meticulously maintained and restored.

Among the most iconic structures is the Cathedral of St. John the Baptist, noted for its remarkable French Gothic architecture and breathtaking interior. Another significant building is the Mercer-Williams House, made famous by the book and movie "Midnight in the Garden of Good and Evil." The Juliette Gordon Low Birthplace, home to the founder of the Girl Scouts of the USA, also draws numerous visitors.

Walking tours of the district are a popular way to soak in the rich history and beautiful sights. These tours often include visits to historic homes, churches, and museums, offering insights into the lives of the people who built and lived in these magnificent structures. Carriage rides and trolley tours are also available for those who prefer a more leisurely exploration of the area.

The Savannah Historic District is not only about history. It is a vibrant neighborhood bustling with activity, home to boutique shops, art galleries, quaint cafes, and some of Savannah's best restaurants. The area comes alive particularly during the annual Savannah Music Festival and the Savannah Film Festival, which attract cultural enthusiasts from around the world.

2. Fort Pulaski National Monument, Tybee Island

Fort Pulaski National Monument, located on Cockspur Island between Savannah and Tybee Island, Georgia, is a site steeped in military history and architectural innovation. Named after Count Casimir Pulaski, the Polish hero who died during the Siege of Savannah in the American Revolutionary War, this fort is a significant monument to the changing nature of military defense technology.

Constructed following the War of 1812, Fort Pulaski was built as part of the United States' coastal fortification system. It was considered invincible with walls over 7 feet thick and capable of withstanding any attack. However, during the Civil War, the fort was famously seized by Union forces in 1862 during the Battle of Fort Pulaski. The Union army used rifled cannon for the first time in history, which could penetrate the fort's formerly impenetrable walls, effectively changing military defense tactics worldwide.

Today, Fort Pulaski operates as a national monument, open to the public for exploration. Visitors can tour the well-preserved fortifications, including the massive brick walls and moat, gaining insights into the 19th-century fortress construction techniques and military life during the Civil War. The fort also offers a variety of educational programs, including daily interpretive talks, musket and cannon demonstrations, and guided tours that delve deep into the fort's strategic significance and the details of its capture.

The area surrounding Fort Pulaski is a haven for wildlife and offers a range of outdoor activities. The monument is surrounded by tidal marshes, mud flats, and open waters that are home to a variety of wildlife, including migratory birds and native plant species. Nature trails and bird watching spots around the monument allow visitors to appreciate the natural beauty of the Georgia coast in addition to its historical significance.

Fort Pulaski National Monument not only provides a fascinating look at a pivotal moment in military history but also offers a picturesque setting that highlights the natural beauty and ecological diversity of the area. It is a place where history and nature intersect, offering a rich educational and recreational experience for visitors.

3. Tybee Island, near Savannah

Tybee Island, located just 18 miles east of Savannah, is a quintessential southern beach town that offers a laid-back coastal lifestyle combined with rich historical heritage. Known as Savannah's beach, this small barrier island boasts a wide, three-mile-long beach that is popular for sunbathing, swimming, and a variety of water sports.

Tybee Island's charm is not just in its sandy shores but also in its colorful character and history. The island is home to the historic Tybee Island Light Station, one of the oldest and most intact lighthouses in America, having been guiding mariners safe entrance into the Savannah River since 1736. Visitors can climb the 178 steps to the top for panoramic views of the Atlantic Ocean and the surrounding landscapes.

The island's strategic location has also played a significant role in American history, evidenced by Fort Screven, which was an important military outpost during the Spanish-American War, World War I, and World War II. Today, several of the fort's beautifully preserved buildings house museums and provide a glimpse into the island's military past.

Beyond its historical attractions, Tybee Island is known for its vibrant local scene and community events. The island hosts annual festivals like the Tybee Pirate Fest, which sees locals and visitors alike dressing up as pirates for parades, family-friendly activities, and live music. The Tybee Island Marine Science Center offers interactive exhibits and coastal programs designed to educate visitors about the region's marine and coastal ecosystems.

With its inviting beaches, historical sites, and lively local culture, Tybee Island offers a perfect blend of relaxation and entertainment. Whether it's exploring the island's history, participating in water activities, or simply enjoying the laid-back atmosphere, Tybee Island is an ideal destination for a day trip or a long vacation near Savannah.

4.   Sapelo Island Visitor Center, Sapelo Island

Sapelo Island, accessible only by boat, lies about sixty miles south of Savannah and is a captivating blend of natural beauty, deep historical roots, and cultural significance. The Sapelo Island Visitor Center, located in the mainland town of Meridian, serves as the gateway to this unique barrier island, offering insights and access to one of Georgia's best-kept secrets.

Visitors to Sapelo Island are first introduced to its rich history and diverse ecology at the Visitor Center, where interactive displays and exhibits provide an overview of the island's cultural heritage and natural environment. The center offers guided tours that allow visitors to explore the island's vibrant ecosystem, which includes salt marshes, beaches, and maritime forests.

One of the most intriguing aspects of Sapelo Island is the Hog Hammock Community, one of the few remaining Gullah-Geechee communities in the South. The descendants of enslaved West Africans have retained much of their African heritage and traditions, which is evident in their language, crafts, and culinary practices. Tours of Hog Hammock provide a rare glimpse into the living history and culture of the Gullah-Geechee people.

Sapelo Island is also home to the Reynolds Mansion, an elegant estate once owned by tobacco heir R.J. Reynolds, and now operated by the State of Georgia as a guest house and event venue. The mansion is an example of the island's storied past and offers a look at its luxurious mid-20th-century life.

The natural landscapes of Sapelo Island are as compelling as its human history. The island features pristine beaches, such as Nanny Goat Beach, untouched by commercial development, offering peaceful solitude and stunning natural beauty. The Sapelo Island National Estuarine Research Reserve provides a protected space for research and education on coastal ecosystems.

The Sapelo Island Visitor Center and its tours offer a comprehensive introduction to the unique historical, cultural, and natural treasures of Sapelo Island, making it a must-visit for anyone interested in exploring Georgia's rich coastal heritage and unspoiled natural environments.

5.   Fort King George Historic Site, Darien

Fort King George Historic Site in Darien, Georgia, stands as a testament to the earliest British military presence on the Georgia coast. Established in 1721, three decades before the founding of Savannah, this fort was strategically positioned to act as a buffer against Spanish incursions from the south and protect the burgeoning British interests in the lucrative North American colonies. Today, the site offers visitors a glimpse into the harsh realities of colonial military life and the complex historical dynamics of the area.

The fort, originally built from cypress and pine logs, was designed to house a garrison of British troops tasked with overseeing and protecting Britain's southern frontier. However, the fort's life was short-lived; due to rampant disease, harsh conditions, and its remote location, it was abandoned by 1727. It wasn't until the 1980s that the site was reconstructed based on extensive archaeological studies, allowing visitors to see a historically accurate replica of the original fort.

Visitors to Fort King George Historic Site can explore various structures within the fort, including the barracks, blockhouses, and a fascinating museum that showcases artifacts recovered from the site. These artifacts, ranging from musket balls and pottery shards to personal items like buttons and coins, provide insight into the daily lives of the soldiers stationed here.

One of the most engaging aspects of the Fort King George experience is the series of live demonstrations conducted by staff dressed in period costumes. These demonstrations, which include musket firings, cooking exhibitions, and woodworking, bring the history of the fort to life in a vivid and interactive manner.

In addition to the fort itself, the site encompasses a beautiful stretch of marshland along the Altamaha River, featuring a scenic boardwalk that offers views of the local flora and fauna. This natural setting not only provides a serene backdrop to the historical site but also highlights the strategic importance of the location for controlling river access.

6.   Hofwyl-Broadfield Plantation, Brunswick

Hofwyl-Broadfield Plantation, located near Brunswick, Georgia, offers visitors a poignant look into the region's antebellum past and its transformation through time. This historic rice plantation, established in the early 19th century, remained in the same family for over 150 years before becoming a state historic site. Today, it serves as a vital link to understanding the economic, social, and environmental aspects of the coastal South's plantation culture.

The centerpiece of Hofwyl-Broadfield Plantation is the magnificent plantation house, built in the Greek Revival style typical of the period. Furnished with original family antiques, the house has been preserved to reflect the lifestyle of the plantation's owners through various generations, from the height of the rice cultivation era to its decline after the Civil War.

Visitors can tour the house and the surrounding outbuildings, including the dairy, barn, and ice house, to get a fuller picture of plantation life. The onsite museum displays a collection of silver, photographs, and documents that further illustrate the family's history and the operation of the plantation.

Perhaps most significantly, Hofwyl-Broadfield Plantation offers insights into the lives of the enslaved Africans who worked the rice fields. Interpretive signs and guided tours discuss the contributions and hardships of these individuals, whose labor was central to the plantation's operation and profitability. This critical perspective ensures a balanced understanding of the site's history.

The plantation is set against the backdrop of Georgia's stunning coastal scenery, with majestic live oaks and Spanish moss framing views of the former rice fields, now lush wetlands. These fields are traversed by a network of trails that allow visitors to explore the area's natural beauty and observe the local wildlife.

7.   Sea Island Resort, Sea Island

Sea Island Resort on Sea Island, Georgia, is a luxury retreat known for its gracious service, elegant settings, and a plethora of activities that cater to high-end travelers looking for a unique and sophisticated getaway. Nestled on the Georgia coast, this private island resort combines natural beauty with luxurious amenities, creating an exclusive haven for relaxation and recreation.

The resort features two main accommodations: The Cloister at Sea Island and The Lodge at Sea Island Golf Club. The Cloister exudes old-world charm with its Spanish Mediterranean architecture, beautiful gardens, and refined interiors. The Lodge, reminiscent of an English country manor, offers stunning views of the Atlantic Ocean and the resort's championship golf courses. Both provide luxurious accommodations, exceptional service, and access to a wide range of amenities.

Sea Island is renowned for its golf offerings, including three championship golf courses that challenge and delight golfers of all skill levels. The courses are known for their scenic vistas and meticulous landscaping, and they have hosted numerous prestigious tournaments, enhancing the resort's reputation as a premier golf destination.

Beyond golf, Sea Island Resort offers a variety of other activities. Guests can enjoy a state-of-the-art spa that offers a wide range of treatments designed to rejuvenate and relax. Outdoor enthusiasts will appreciate the extensive recreational activities available, including horseback riding, kayaking, sailing, and fishing. The resort also provides a range of children's programs, making it an ideal choice for family vacations.

Dining at Sea Island is an experience in itself, with several restaurants offering everything from casual to gourmet fare. Using fresh, local ingredients, including seafood caught directly from the surrounding waters, the resort's chefs create dishes that are as delightful to the palate as they are to the eye.

8.   St. Simons Island Lighthouse Museum, St. Simons Island

The St. Simons Island Lighthouse Museum is one of the most iconic landmarks on St. Simons Island, Georgia, and a focal point of historical interest in the region. Located near the village and pier, the lighthouse is a working lighthouse from the late 19th century and is managed by the Coastal Georgia Historical Society. It provides visitors with a rare opportunity to step back in time and experience maritime history up close.

Visitors to the St. Simons Island Lighthouse Museum can climb the 129 steps to the top of the lighthouse for panoramic views of the Atlantic Ocean, the surrounding barrier islands, and the mainland. The climb is worth the effort, offering one of the best vantage points on the island for breathtaking coastal scenery.

The accompanying A.W. Jones Heritage Center serves as the visitor center and museum, providing exhibits on the history of the St. Simons Lighthouse and the maritime heritage of the area. Artifacts, photographs, and interactive displays tell the story of the lighthouse keepers, their daily lives, and the evolution of maritime navigation. The museum also explores the broader history of St. Simons Island, from its early Native American inhabitants through its development as a strategic point in coastal Georgia.

The lighthouse and museum are not only significant for their historical and educational value; they also play an active role in the community. The site hosts numerous events throughout the year, including concerts, lectures, and community gatherings, which underscore its status as a cultural hub on the island.

For those interested in history, architecture, or simply looking for a picturesque setting, the St. Simons Island Lighthouse Museum offers a compelling glimpse into the maritime past of Georgia, making it a cherished landmark and a must-visit destination on the coast.

9.   Brunswick Old Town Historic District, Brunswick

The Brunswick Old Town Historic District, located in the heart of Brunswick, Georgia, is a charming and historically rich area that offers a glimpse into the city's past through its well-preserved architecture and old-world charm. Established in 1771 and laid out in a formal grid pattern similar to Savannah and Philadelphia, Brunswick is one of the oldest cities in Georgia, and its historic district is a testament to its long and varied history.

Covering several city blocks, the Old Town Historic District features a variety of architectural styles that span several centuries, including Victorian, Queen Anne, and Colonial Revival. These historic buildings house a mix of residences, businesses, and cultural institutions, making the district not only a hub of architectural beauty but also a vibrant center of community life.

One of the standout features of the district is the Ritz Theatre, originally built in the 1890s and restored as a vibrant performing arts venue. The theatre today hosts a variety of performances, including live music, theater, and dance, as well as films and lectures. It serves as a cultural anchor for the district and a gathering place for the community.

The streets of the historic district are lined with mature oak trees draped with Spanish moss, adding to the area's scenic beauty and Southern charm. Visitors can take a leisurely stroll along Newcastle Street, the main thoroughfare, which is dotted with antique shops, art galleries, cozy cafes, and gourmet restaurants. This street is particularly lively during the monthly First Friday events, when local businesses stay open late, and the community comes together to enjoy live music, food, and street vendors.

The Brunswick Old Town Historic District is not only a place to explore the rich tapestry of architectural styles and historical layers but also a place to enjoy the laid-back lifestyle and friendly atmosphere of a Southern city. Whether you're a history buff, an architecture enthusiast, or simply looking for a pleasant place to wander and relax, Brunswick's historic district offers a delightful and enriching experience.

10. Driftwood Beach, Jekyll Island

Driftwood Beach, located on the northern end of Jekyll Island, Georgia, offers one of the most unique and picturesque landscapes in the region. Known for its surreal scenery dotted with weathered and bleached driftwood trees, this beach provides a striking contrast to the typical sandy beach and palm tree landscape people expect from a coastal retreat.

The hauntingly beautiful driftwood, remnants of maritime forests, provides an evocative backdrop that is popular with photographers and nature lovers. Over time, erosion has claimed the trees that once stood tall behind the dunes, leaving behind an otherworldly scene that captivates visitors with its stark, natural beauty.

Driftwood Beach is not only a place for scenic walks and photo opportunities; it is also an excellent spot for bird watching, fishing, and picnicking. The beach's orientation makes it an ideal location to watch the sunrise over the Atlantic, offering peaceful solitude and a chance to reconnect with nature.

This beach's unique charm also makes it a favored spot for romantic getaways and is a popular destination for weddings. Couples often choose Driftwood Beach for its dramatic landscape and the unforgettable ambiance it provides for their special day.

Despite its beauty, Driftwood Beach serves as a stark reminder of the dynamic and ever-changing nature of coastal environments. It highlights the impact of natural processes on our landscapes and serves as a natural classroom for visitors interested in coastal ecology and conservation.

Whether you're looking for a place to reflect and unwind or a stunning natural setting for photography, Driftwood Beach offers a unique and memorable experience that stands out among Georgia's coastal attractions.

11.   Jekyll Island Historic District, Jekyll Island

Jekyll Island Historic District, nestled on Jekyll Island, Georgia, is a captivating area that transports visitors back to a time when the island served as an exclusive winter retreat for America's wealthiest families. Known as the "Millionaires' Village," this historic district comprises a collection of over thirty buildings that include opulent cottages, a chapel, and the grand Jekyll Island Club Hotel, which was the center of social life for the elite vacationers.

Established in the late 19th century, the Jekyll Island Club was originally developed as a private hunting and recreational club. Members included prominent figures such as J.P. Morgan, William Rockefeller, and Joseph Pulitzer. Today, the beautifully restored Jekyll Island Club Hotel operates as a full-service resort, offering guests a taste of Gilded Age luxury with modern amenities.

The historic district is more than just a collection of beautiful old buildings. It offers a variety of cultural and recreational activities, including tours of the historic cottages, art exhibitions, and musical performances. Visitors can explore the district by foot, bicycle, or guided trolley tours, which provide insights into the fascinating history of the island and its transformation from an exclusive social club to a state park open to the public.

The district also includes the Faith Chapel, notable for its beautiful stained glass windows, including one signed by Louis Comfort Tiffany. Another significant building is the Indian Mound Cottage, once owned by William Rockefeller, which exemplifies the luxurious lifestyle of the island's former inhabitants.

Today, the Jekyll Island Historic District is not only a window into a bygone era but also a vibrant part of the community that hosts weddings, conferences, and social gatherings. Its blend of historical significance, architectural beauty, and coastal charm makes it a must-visit destination for anyone traveling to Georgia's Golden Isles.

12. Cumberland Island National Seashore, St. Marys

Cumberland Island National Seashore, located just off the coast of St. Marys, Georgia, is a spectacular and pristine natural area protected by the National Park Service. As the largest and southernmost barrier island in Georgia, Cumberland Island offers over 17 miles of secluded sandy beaches, dense maritime forests, and expansive salt marshes.

The island is accessible only by ferry, which helps preserve its wilderness state. Once on the island, visitors can explore a variety of landscapes that are home to a rich array of wildlife, including wild horses that roam freely, as well as armadillos, deer, and numerous bird species. The island's diverse ecosystems make it an ideal spot for nature lovers interested in hiking, bird watching, and wildlife photography.

One of the highlights of Cumberland Island is the Dungeness Ruins, the remains of a once-grand estate built by Thomas Carnegie, brother of steel magnate Andrew Carnegie. The ruins and the surrounding grounds tell a story of the island's past wealth and grandeur. Nearby, the Cumberland Island National Seashore Museum in St. Marys offers additional insights into the island's natural, cultural, and historical background.

Camping is available on the island, with several designated campsites that range from developed areas with facilities to wilderness campsites that offer a more primitive and intimate experience with nature. Camping on Cumberland Island provides a unique opportunity to experience the serene beauty of the island under the stars.

Cumberland Island National Seashore is not only a place of breathtaking natural beauty but also a site of conservation and ecological research. It is a dynamic landscape that continually evolves, shaped by the natural forces of wind, water, and time. For those seeking a tranquil retreat from modern life, Cumberland Island offers a rare blend of adventure, history, and solitude, making it one of the most cherished natural landmarks in the Southeast United States.

13.   Okefenokee Swamp, Waycross

The Okefenokee Swamp, located near Waycross, Georgia, is one of North America's most unspoiled and mysterious natural habitats. This extensive 700 square mile peat-filled wetland lies at the Georgia-Florida border and is one of the oldest and most well-preserved freshwater systems in America. Its name, derived from the Seminole language, means "land of trembling earth," aptly describing the swampy terrain where the peat deposits cover the water and tremble underfoot.

The Okefenokee Swamp is renowned for its rich biodiversity. It is home to over 400 species of animals, including American alligators, black bears, hundreds of bird species, and numerous fish and amphibian species. This makes it an exceptional destination for wildlife enthusiasts and bird watchers who can observe these species in their natural habitat. The swamp's diverse ecosystems, which range from cypress forests and marshes to scrub-shrub areas, also support a variety of plant life, including carnivorous plants like the pitcher plant and sundew.

Visitors to the Okefenokee Swamp can explore this vast wetland through guided boat tours, canoeing, and kayaking. These excursions offer close encounters with the swamp's wildlife and a firsthand look at its unique vegetation. The swamp's water trails and boardwalks allow visitors to navigate through dense cypress forests and eerie blackwater lakes where the reflections of old-growth trees darken the waters.

The Okefenokee National Wildlife Refuge, which encompasses much of the swamp, provides numerous educational opportunities through its visitor center. Here, guests can learn about the swamp's ecological importance, its cultural history, and ongoing conservation efforts. The refuge also offers ranger-led programs that delve deeper into the swamp's natural history and provide tips for spotting wildlife.

For those seeking a more immersive experience, several camping options are available within the refuge, including established campgrounds and more primitive backcountry sites accessible only by canoe. Camping in the Okefenokee Swamp is an unforgettable experience, offering serene evenings surrounded by the sounds of nocturnal wildlife and starlit skies.

14.   Stephen C. Foster State Park, Fargo

Located in the heart of the Okefenokee Swamp near Fargo, Georgia, Stephen C. Foster State Park is a gateway to the wild beauty of one of America's most intriguing natural habitats. Named after the famous songwriter who penned "Old Folks at Home," the park serves as a primary access point to the western portion of the Okefenokee National Wildlife Refuge, offering a range of activities and experiences that highlight the swamp's unique environment.

Stephen C. Foster State Park is especially popular with nature enthusiasts who come to explore its lush landscapes and diverse wildlife. The park offers guided boat tours that venture deep into the swamp, providing opportunities to see alligators, turtles, and a variety of bird species in their natural surroundings. For those who prefer a more hands-on approach, canoe and kayak rentals are available, allowing visitors to paddle along the swamp's waterways at their own pace.

The park is also known for its excellent fishing opportunities. The still waters of the Okefenokee are home to several species of fish, including catfish, bass, and bluegill, making it a favorite spot for anglers. Fishing can be enjoyed from the banks or by boat, and the park's fishing dock is a convenient place to cast a line.

For visitors interested in hiking, the park features a boardwalk that winds through the swamp, offering a safe and accessible way to explore the area's scenic beauty. The boardwalk ends at an observation tower that provides panoramic views of the surrounding wetlands, a perfect spot for photography and bird watching.

Camping at Stephen C. Foster State Park is an experience like no other, with options ranging from fully equipped cabins to primitive campsites. Nighttime in the park offers a symphony of sounds from nocturnal animals, and the lack of light pollution makes for spectacular stargazing.

The park also plays an educational role, with a visitor center that offers exhibits on the Okefenokee Swamp's ecosystem and history. These displays provide valuable insights into the importance of preserving such a unique environment.

15. Wild Adventures Theme Park, Valdosta

Wild Adventures Theme Park in Valdosta, Georgia, is a vibrant and action-packed destination that offers a blend of exciting rides, live entertainment, and exotic animals, making it a unique attraction in the South. Spread across 170 acres, the park features a combination of amusement park thrills and a zoo that hosts hundreds of animals from around the world.

Thrill-seekers can enjoy a variety of roller coasters and rides at Wild Adventures. Some of the park's most popular coasters include the Boomerang, a thrilling coaster that loops riders forward and backward through corkscrews and loops, and the Cheetah, a wooden coaster known for its high-speed drops and twists. For younger visitors and families, the park offers gentler rides and attractions, ensuring that guests of all ages can have a fun and memorable experience.

In addition to the rides, Wild Adventures provides a close-up look at exotic wildlife in naturalistic habitats. The park's zoo features over 500 animals, including lions, tigers, and elephants. Guests can attend educational shows that allow them to learn about the habits and habitats of these animals, emphasizing conservation and wildlife protection.

Wild Adventures also hosts a variety of shows and concerts throughout the year. These live performances include music concerts, featuring popular bands and artists, and themed seasonal events like Halloween and Christmas specials, which transform the park with decorations and themed activities.

With its wide array of attractions and events, Wild Adventures Theme Park is more than just a theme park; it's a comprehensive family entertainment center. It combines the excitement of an amusement park with the educational and interactive experiences of a zoo, making it a popular destination for families, thrill-seekers, and animal lovers alike.

16.   Pebble Hill Plantation, Thomasville

Pebble Hill Plantation in Thomasville, Georgia, is a historic estate that encapsulates the tradition and beauty of the Old South. Situated on over 3,000 acres of land, this sprawling plantation dates back to the mid-19th century and was part of the Red Hills Region's once-thriving plantation community. Today, Pebble Hill offers visitors a glimpse into the grandeur of Southern plantation life, showcasing classical architecture, stunning gardens, and a rich collection of art and antiques.

The main house at Pebble Hill is an architectural marvel, redesigned in the classical revival style in the early 20th century. Visitors can tour the house and explore its beautifully preserved interiors, which are furnished with an impressive collection of original antiques, artworks, and decorative items that reflect the lifestyle of its former inhabitants. Each room tells a story, adorned with pieces from around the world, demonstrating the wealth and cultural interests of the plantation's owners.

Outside, the grounds of Pebble Hill are just as impressive as the interior. The estate features a variety of gardens that bloom year-round, including formal gardens with neatly trimmed hedges and casual flower gardens that attract a variety of birds and butterflies. Guests can take guided tours or wander the paths on their own to enjoy the tranquil beauty of these well-maintained landscapes.

Pebble Hill Plantation also serves as a cultural center, hosting educational programs and community events, including outdoor concerts, art shows, and seasonal festivals. Additionally, the plantation operates as a venue for weddings and private events, offering a picturesque setting that exemplifies Southern elegance and charm.

With its rich history, stunning architecture, and beautiful gardens, Pebble Hill Plantation remains a testament to the heritage and lifestyle of the South's plantation era. It provides visitors with a fascinating insight into a bygone era, preserved amidst the natural beauty of Thomasville.

17. Radium Springs Gardens, Albany

Radium Springs Gardens, located just outside Albany, Georgia, is one of the state's seven natural wonders and a site steeped in both beauty and mystery. Known for its vividly blue waters, the springs pump 70,000 gallons of clear, 68-degree water each minute into a beautiful pool that was once the site of a popular resort in the early 20th century.

The history of Radium Springs dates back to the 1920s and 1930s when it was home to a flourishing casino and resort that attracted visitors from all over the country. The casino was renowned for its elegant architecture and the supposedly therapeutic properties of the spring water. Although the original casino building was destroyed by a flood in 1994, the site has been preserved as a historical landmark and transformed into a botanical garden that maintains the grandeur and allure of its heyday.

Today, Radium Springs Gardens is a sanctuary for both nature lovers and history enthusiasts. The gardens surrounding the springs are meticulously landscaped and feature a mix of native and exotic plants that thrive in the warm Georgia climate. Paved walkways wind through the gardens, offering serene views of the spring and the surrounding flora. The area is also equipped with gazebos and benches where visitors can sit back and enjoy the peaceful environment.

While swimming in the springs is no longer allowed, the site remains a popular destination for its picturesque scenery and the cooling mist that rises off the waters. Educational signage around the park provides insights into the natural and cultural history of the springs, offering visitors a glimpse into the geological forces that created this natural wonder and the historical events that shaped its development.

Radium Springs Gardens is not just a place of natural beauty but also a community gathering space, hosting various events and activities throughout the year, including outdoor concerts, educational programs, and environmental conservation efforts. It stands as a testament to the region's rich heritage and natural beauty, making it a cherished landmark in the Albany area.

18.   Chehaw Park, Albany

Chehaw Park in Albany, Georgia, is a uniquely comprehensive natural area that includes a zoo, recreational facilities, and a nature park. Spanning over 800 acres, Chehaw offers a multitude of activities and experiences, making it a versatile destination for visitors looking for a mix of adventure, wildlife, and relaxation.

At the heart of Chehaw Park is the zoo, officially known as the Chehaw Wild Animal Park. Accredited by the Association of Zoos and Aquariums (AZA), the zoo is committed to the conservation and protection of wild animals, providing a home to over 200 animals from around the world. Species range from African black rhinos to North American bobcats, and the zoo's layout is designed to offer visitors an immersive experience that mimics the animals' natural habitats.

Beyond the zoo, Chehaw Park boasts an extensive network of recreational facilities that cater to a variety of interests and age groups. The park offers miles of biking and hiking trails that wind through diverse ecosystems, including wetlands, forests, and prairies. For more organized sports, there are facilities for BMX biking, disc golf, and a skate park.

Chehaw also features a large play park designed with natural materials and themed after native wildlife, making it an ideal spot for families. The park's camping grounds provide another layer of adventure, offering both traditional campsites and unique camping experiences like yurts, providing options for those who wish to extend their stay and enjoy the natural beauty of the area overnight.

Throughout the year, Chehaw Park hosts a variety of events and educational programs that engage the community and visitors. These range from native plant sales and wildlife presentations to large-scale events like festivals and races, all designed to promote environmental awareness and community involvement.

Chehaw Park's blend of conservation, recreation, and education makes it a standout destination in Georgia, offering a rich, engaging experience that appeals to nature lovers, thrill-seekers, and families alike.

19. Jefferson Davis Memorial Historic Site, Fitzgerald

The Jefferson Davis Memorial Historic Site in Fitzgerald, Georgia, is a significant historical landmark dedicated to preserving the capture site of Jefferson Davis, the president of the Confederate States of America during the American Civil War. Located near the end of the Civil War in 1865, this site marks the place where Davis was captured by Union troops, effectively ending the Confederate government's attempts to continue the war.

The site features a museum that houses a collection of artifacts related to Davis' capture, including period firearms, photographs, and documents. The museum provides a detailed account of the last days of the Confederacy and the circumstances leading up to Davis' capture. This includes a focus on his flight from Richmond, Virginia, through the southern states, trying to evade Union forces.

Visitors to the Jefferson Davis Memorial Historic Site can also explore the outdoor area, which includes a marked trail to the actual capture site. The trail is lined with interpretive signs that provide historical context and describe the significance of various aspects of the site and its surroundings. The location is preserved much as it was in the 19th century, offering a tangible connection to this pivotal moment in American history.

In addition to exploring the museum and trail, visitors can participate in educational programs and events that the site hosts throughout the year. These programs often include Civil War reenactments, lectures on Civil War history, and memorial services that provide deeper insights into the era and its lasting impacts on American society.

The Jefferson Davis Memorial Historic Site serves as both a resource for historical education and a place of reflection on the complexities of the Civil War and its aftermath. It stands as a reminder of the turbulent times that shaped the United States and the figures who played pivotal roles in its history.

20. General Coffee State Park, Douglas

General Coffee State Park, located near Douglas, Georgia, offers a blend of natural beauty, historical significance, and recreational activities. Named after General John Coffee, a planter, and military leader, the park is part of Georgia's rich agricultural and historical landscape. It covers more than 1,500 acres and features a heritage farm, with log cabins, a barn, and other structures that illustrate the life of 19th-century farmers.

One of the park's main attractions is the Heritage Farm, which has live animals and displays about traditional farming practices. This living history museum allows visitors to step back in time and experience the rural lifestyle of Georgia's past, including demonstrations of farming techniques and crafts like blacksmithing and quilting.

The park's natural features include cypress swamps, sandhills, and pine forests, which provide a habitat for a wide variety of wildlife. Birdwatchers and nature enthusiasts can enjoy the park's extensive network of trails, which offer excellent opportunities to observe birds and other wildlife in their natural settings.

For outdoor recreation, General Coffee State Park offers fishing in its small lakes, horseback riding trails, and a 4-mile hiking trail that winds through the scenic landscape. The park also has facilities for picnicking, camping, and hosting group gatherings, making it a popular destination for families and outdoor enthusiasts.

Throughout the year, General Coffee State Park hosts educational programs and events that focus on environmental conservation, wildlife, and the cultural history of the area. These programs are designed to engage visitors of all ages and provide them with a deeper appreciation of Georgia's natural and cultural heritage.

General Coffee State Park is not just a place for relaxation and recreation but also a venue for learning and discovery, offering a rich experience that combines the joys of the outdoors with the insights of history.

21. Little Ocmulgee State Park and Lodge, McRae

Little Ocmulgee State Park and Lodge, situated near McRae, Georgia, is a sanctuary for nature lovers and outdoor enthusiasts who enjoy a peaceful retreat in the wilderness. This expansive state park, covering over 1,360 acres, features a wide array of natural landscapes, including hardwood forests, a small lake, and the intriguing "Little Ocmulgee" itself—a blackwater river that lends the park its name.

The park is particularly known for its 265-acre lake and its accompanying beach, where visitors can enjoy swimming, fishing, and boating. The lake is a serene spot for anglers seeking bass, bream, and crappie, and its tranquil waters are ideal for kayaking and canoeing. Alongside these water-based activities, Little Ocmulgee boasts an 18-hole Wallace Adams Golf Course, renowned for its challenging layout and scenic beauty. The course is a draw for golfers of all skill levels and is complemented by a pro shop and a clubhouse.

For accommodations, Little Ocmulgee State Park offers a variety of options that cater to different preferences and needs. The lodge at the park provides comfortable hotel-style rooms with modern amenities and beautiful views of the surrounding nature. For those who prefer a more rustic experience, there are facilities for camping and cabins equipped with kitchens and multiple bedrooms, providing a perfect family getaway.

Nature trails are another highlight of Little Ocmulgee State Park. The park features several miles of walking trails, including the 2.6-mile Oak Ridge Trail, which winds through the park's diverse ecosystems. This trail offers excellent opportunities for bird watching and wildlife observation, as the park is home to deer, turkeys, and numerous bird species.

The park also includes a splash pad, mini-golf course, and playgrounds, making it particularly family-friendly. These facilities ensure that children have ample opportunities for play and entertainment during their visit. Throughout the year, Little Ocmulgee State Park hosts a variety of educational and recreational programs, including guided hikes, wildlife presentations, and crafting workshops, which enhance the visitor experience and provide deeper insights into the local environment and its inhabitants.

22. Georgia Veterans State Park, Cordele

Georgia Veterans State Park, located on the shores of Lake Blackshear in Cordele, Georgia, serves as a tribute to the U.S. veterans from the Revolutionary War through the present day. The park combines recreational activities with a military museum and other memorials, offering a unique blend of education and relaxation in a picturesque setting.

The park's museum is dedicated to preserving and displaying military artifacts that span decades of American history. Exhibits include tanks, aircraft, uniforms, and other memorabilia that help visitors understand the experiences and sacrifices of American soldiers in various conflicts. One of the highlights is a beautifully restored B-29A Superfortress and other military aircraft that are displayed on the museum grounds.

In addition to its historical attractions, Georgia Veterans State Park is well known for its recreational offerings. Lake Blackshear, a 8,700-acre lake, provides ample opportunities for fishing, boating, and water sports. The park features a marina where visitors can rent boats or store their own, and there are also fishing piers and a fish cleaning station available for anglers.

The park is also home to a 9-hole golf course that caters to players of all skill levels, offering a relaxing and scenic environment to enjoy a round of golf. For those who prefer land-based activities, there are more than three miles of walking and biking trails that meander through the park's diverse landscapes.

Accommodation options at Georgia Veterans State Park include a resort lodge, cabins, and a campground, all of which provide a comfortable stay amidst the natural beauty of the park. The lodge offers hotel-style rooms with views of Lake Blackshear, while the cabins and campgrounds provide more rustic accommodations for families and groups.

Georgia Veterans State Park hosts several events throughout the year, including patriotic ceremonies on holidays such as Memorial Day and Veterans Day, which draw crowds from across the region. These events, along with the everyday offerings of the park, make it a significant site for both recreation and reflection, honoring the legacy of American veterans while providing a multitude of activities for visitors.

23.   Andersonville National Historic Site, Andersonville

Andersonville National Historic Site, located in Andersonville, Georgia, preserves the site of Camp Sumter military prison, one of the most notorious Confederate prisoner-of-war camps during the American Civil War. Today, the site serves as a memorial to all American prisoners of war throughout the nation's history, offering a poignant reminder of the harsh realities of conflict.

The history of Andersonville is sobering. During its 14 months of operation, the prison confined more than 45,000 Union soldiers, of whom nearly 13,000 died due to starvation, disease, and poor treatment. The conditions at Andersonville were among the worst of any prison in the Civil War, with severe overcrowding, inadequate food supplies, and minimal shelter from the elements.

Visitors to Andersonville National Historic Site can explore the prison site, which is outlined by a series of posts marking the original stockade boundaries. A reconstructed section of the stockade wall provides a visual sense of the confinement conditions. The site also features the National Prisoner of War Museum, which offers exhibits that interpret the experiences of prisoners held in various conflicts, emphasizing themes of sacrifice, survival, and memory.

The cemetery at Andersonville, known as the Andersonville National Cemetery, contains the graves of Union prisoners who died at the camp, as well as veterans and their families from later periods. The cemetery is a deeply moving site, with rows of headstones that serve as a somber reminder of the costs of war.

Andersonville National Historic Site offers educational programs, including guided tours and historical demonstrations, that help visitors understand the historical significance of the site and the broader context of the Civil War. The site also hosts annual events, such as memorial ceremonies and history encampments, which contribute to the understanding and honoring of those who suffered and died in prisoner-of-war camps.

The Jimmy Carter National Historic Site, located in Plains, Georgia, celebrates and preserves the legacy of Jimmy Carter, the 39th President of the United States, highlighting his humble beginnings and the values that guided his life and presidency. This historic site encompasses several buildings in Plains that played significant roles in Carter's life and political career.

Visitors to the site can explore Jimmy Carter's boyhood farm, where he grew up during the Great Depression. The farm is restored to its appearance during the 1930s and offers a glimpse into the rural Southern life that shaped Carter's character and future policies. The farm includes the Carter family home, a general store, and other outbuildings, each filled with interactive exhibits that provide insights into the daily challenges and workings of a Depression-era farm.

Another key component of the historic site is the Plains High School, which now serves as the visitor center and museum. The museum features exhibits on Carter's presidency and his significant achievements, including his efforts in peacekeeping and human rights, which earned him a Nobel Peace Prize in 2002. Personal artifacts, photographs, and multimedia displays tell the story of his journey from a small-town peanut farmer to a world leader.

The Carter Compound, where President Carter and his wife, Rosalynn, have lived for most of their lives, is also part of the historic site. While it is not open for public tours, it can be viewed from a distance, and it represents the deep connection the Carters maintain with their hometown.

The site also includes the Plains Train Depot, which served as Carter's campaign headquarters during the 1976 presidential election. The depot features exhibits about the campaign and the electoral process, highlighting how Carter's grassroots campaigning methods led to his unexpected victory.

The Jimmy Carter National Historic Site not only honors the life and work of Jimmy Carter but also serves as an educational resource that offers profound insights into American political history, presidential campaigns, and the importance of community and humble beginnings.

North Georgia and Mountains

1.   North Georgia Premium Outlets, Dawsonville

North Georgia Premium Outlets, located in Dawsonville, Georgia, is a shopper's paradise nestled in the scenic foothills of the North Georgia mountains. As one of the premier shopping destinations in the region, this outlet center offers an exceptional blend of luxury brands and mainstream retailers at discounted prices, attracting both local residents and tourists looking for quality shopping experiences.

Spanning over 481,000 square feet, North Georgia Premium Outlets features more than 140 designer and name-brand outlet stores. Shoppers can explore a wide range of high-end brands such as Michael Kors, Coach, Polo Ralph Lauren, and Burberry, alongside popular brands like Nike, Gap, and Levi's. This diverse mix ensures that all visitors can find something to suit their tastes and budgets, whether they are searching for the latest fashion trends, outdoor gear, or children's clothing.

The architecture of the outlet mall pays homage to the region's natural beauty, with its design reflecting the rustic charm of a mountain lodge, featuring stone facades and timber beams. The open-air layout of the center allows shoppers to enjoy the beautiful, often temperate weather of North Georgia as they move from store to store, enhancing the overall shopping experience.

In addition to shopping, North Georgia Premium Outlets offers a variety of dining options. These range from fast food to sit-down restaurants, providing plenty of choices for shoppers looking to take a break and refuel. Seasonal food carts and kiosks also offer snacks and drinks, perfect for those on the go.

The outlet center is not just about shopping and dining; it hosts a variety of events throughout the year. Seasonal sales events, holiday celebrations, and special promotions add an extra layer of excitement for shoppers. For families, the center often organizes activities and entertainment that keep children engaged and entertained.

2. Amicalola Falls State Park, Dawsonville

Amicalola Falls State Park, located in Dawsonville, Georgia, is a true gem of the state park system, renowned for its stunning natural beauty and outdoor recreational opportunities. The park is named after Amicalola Falls, a breathtaking 729-foot waterfall that is one of the tallest cascading waterfalls east of the Mississippi River. This majestic waterfall is the centerpiece of the park and a must-see attraction for visitors.

Spanning over 829 acres, the park offers a variety of activities that cater to all levels of outdoor enthusiasts. The most popular activity is hiking, with numerous trails that range from easy walks to more challenging hikes. The most famed trail is the Appalachian Approach Trail, which extends 8.5 miles from the park to Springer Mountain, the southern terminus of the Appalachian Trail. This trail offers hikers spectacular views of the falls and the surrounding Appalachian Mountains.

For those looking for a less strenuous way to enjoy the views, a series of staircases adjacent to the waterfall provides a direct route to see the falls up close. There are several observation decks along the way, allowing visitors to pause and appreciate the power and beauty of the falling water at various points.

Amicalola Falls State Park also offers a variety of accommodations, from a modern lodge with comfortable rooms and stunning mountain views to cabins tucked away in quiet woods and a campground that provides a more rustic outdoor experience. These accommodations make the park a perfect retreat for weekend getaways or longer vacations.

In addition to hiking and lodging, the park features educational programs that include guided hikes, bird watching tours, and survivalist skills workshops, which are especially popular among families and school groups. These programs are designed to enhance visitors' understanding of the natural world and to teach valuable outdoor skills.

Amicalola Falls State Park is not only a place of incredible natural beauty but also a destination for adventure and relaxation. It offers a peaceful yet invigorating environment where visitors can escape the hustle and bustle of everyday life and reconnect with nature.

3. Dahlonega Gold Museum State Historic Site, Dahlonega

The Dahlonega Gold Museum State Historic Site, located in the heart of Dahlonega, Georgia, offers visitors a fascinating glimpse into the history of the first major gold rush in the United States. Housed in the restored 1836 Lumpkin County Courthouse, one of the oldest courthouse buildings in Georgia, the museum chronicles the history of gold mining in the area, which predates the more famous California Gold Rush by almost two decades.

The museum's exhibits provide a comprehensive overview of how gold mining influenced the development of the region and the state. Visitors can view a variety of artifacts from the gold mining era, including gold nuggets, mining equipment, and historical documents. One of the highlights is a film that recounts the story of the gold rush through the experiences of miners and local townspeople.

Interactive displays throughout the museum explain the processes of prospecting, mining, and minting gold. One of the most interesting aspects of Dahlonega's gold history is the establishment of the United States Mint branch in the town, which minted gold coins from 1838 to 1861. Replicas of these coins are on display at the museum, along with the original minting equipment.

The Dahlonega Gold Museum is not only about the past; it also educates visitors about the geology of gold, and how it continues to play a role in the local economy. The museum serves as an educational resource for students and historians alike and provides insight into the cultural heritage of the Appalachian region.

In addition to exploring the museum, visitors to Dahlonega can experience the legacy of the gold rush throughout the town. Several local businesses offer gold panning activities where visitors can try their hand at panning for gold in streams, much like the original prospectors. These experiences, combined with the museum's educational exhibits, provide a full picture of Dahlonega's gold rush era.

The Dahlonega Gold Museum State Historic Site is a cultural and educational treasure, offering visitors a unique opportunity to explore a significant period in Georgia's history.

4.   Consolidated Gold Mine, Dahlonega

The Consolidated Gold Mine, located in Dahlonega, Georgia, offers a rare and fascinating look into the world of gold mining. Established during the late 19th century, this was one of the largest gold mining operations east of the Mississippi River. Today, it operates as a historical site offering guided tours that delve deep into the mine's tunnels, some of the oldest in the state.

Visitors to the Consolidated Gold Mine can embark on a journey back in time to experience the life of a gold miner in the late 1800s. The underground tour leads guests through the mine's expansive network of tunnels, where experienced guides recount tales of the grueling work and the quest for gold that drove men to dig ever deeper into the earth. The cool, damp tunnels are lined with veins of quartz, and the walls still glitter with traces of gold, giving visitors a real sense of the mine's history and significance.

In addition to the underground tour, Consolidated Gold Mine offers gold panning and gemstone mining, which are popular with families and school groups. Visitors can sift through ore at the mine's sluice boxes to find their own gold and gemstones, just as prospectors did over a century ago. This hands-on activity not only provides fun and excitement but also teaches valuable lessons about geology and mining techniques.

The mine also features a museum that displays artifacts, photographs, and tools used in the original mining operations. These exhibits provide a deeper understanding of the technological advances and human stories behind the gold mining industry. The museum shop offers a variety of souvenirs, including gold nuggets and gemstones, gold panning kits, and educational materials.

Consolidated Gold Mine is more than just a historical site; it's an educational adventure that offers a glimpse into Georgia's rich mining heritage. It attracts visitors from all over the country, drawn by the chance to explore the underground tunnels and pan for gold. Whether you're a history enthusiast, a family looking for an interactive experience, or simply curious about the gold mining process, the Consolidated Gold Mine provides a memorable and enriching experience.

5.   Georgia Wine Country Tours, Dahlonega

Dahlonega, often heralded as the heart of Georgia Wine Country, offers a captivating experience for wine enthusiasts through its comprehensive Georgia Wine Country Tours. Nestled in the foothills of the North Georgia mountains, this region has fostered a vibrant viticulture that benefits from the rich mountain soil and the favorable climate, making it a prime location for producing a variety of high-quality wines.

Georgia Wine Country Tours provide an immersive experience, showcasing the best of what Dahlonega's wineries have to offer. These tours are designed not only to taste exceptional wines but also to educate visitors about the wine-making process from vine to bottle.

A typical tour might begin at a boutique winery where visitors can learn about the intricacies of vineyard management and the art of small-batch wine production. This could be followed by a visit to a larger, more established winery where the focus shifts to advanced wine-making technologies and broader distribution strategies. Tastings usually accompany each winery visit, allowing guests to appreciate the unique characteristics of each wine, including local favorites like the European-style red and white wines that have garnered national acclaim.

In addition to wine tasting, many tours offer gourmet dining options that pair exquisite local cuisine with the perfect wine, enhancing the culinary experience. These meals are often set against picturesque backdrops of rolling hills and expansive vineyards, adding a romantic ambiance to the dining experience.

Georgia Wine Country Tours are more than just wine tastings; they are a celebration of local culture and the artistry of wine-making. They often include educational components, such as discussions on the history of Georgia wine and its impact on the local economy, making them a holistic experience for both novice enthusiasts and connoisseurs alike.

For those looking to delve deeper into Georgia's wine culture, Dahlonega offers the Annual Wine Tasting Event, which attracts wine lovers from across the country. This event is a perfect opportunity to sample a wide array of wines and meet other like-minded individuals who share a passion for wine.

6.   Yonah Mountain Vineyards, Cleveland

Nestled at the base of the stunning Yonah Mountain in Cleveland, Georgia, Yonah Mountain Vineyards is a family-owned winery that has quickly become a jewel of the North Georgia wine country. Spanning over 200 acres, with 20 acres dedicated to meticulously cultivated vineyards, this winery is renowned for its commitment to crafting premium wines and its innovative approach to viticulture.

Yonah Mountain Vineyards takes advantage of the mountain's unique microclimate and the fertile soil to produce a variety of grape types, primarily focusing on European varietals like Chardonnay, Merlot, Cabernet Sauvignon, and Petit Verdot. This diverse planting strategy allows the winery to experiment with blends and single varietal wines, pushing the boundaries of traditional winemaking in the region.

Visitors to Yonah Mountain Vineyards can partake in guided tours that provide an in-depth look at the vine-to-bottle process. The tours often include a walk through the vineyards, a visit to the state-of-the-art cellar, and a stop at the cave tasting room – a unique feature that offers a barrel sampling experience deep within a custom-built cave. This immersive experience is not only educational but also gives insights into the complex process of wine aging and flavor development.

The tasting room at Yonah Mountain Vineyards is another highlight, offering panoramic views of the surrounding mountains and vineyards. Here, guests can sample a selection of the winery's current releases and limited edition wines. The knowledgeable staff provides detailed descriptions of each wine, including tasting notes and food pairing suggestions, enhancing the tasting experience.

Yonah Mountain Vineyards also hosts a variety of events throughout the year, including music concerts, wine release parties, and the highly anticipated Crush Fest. This annual event celebrates the harvest season with grape stomping, live music, and wine tasting, attracting visitors from all over to participate in the festivities and celebrate the craft of winemaking.

7. Smithgall Woods State Park, Helen

Smithgall Woods State Park, located just outside Helen, Georgia, is a pristine natural sanctuary known for its untouched beauty and conservation efforts. This park, originally a private retreat of Charles Smithgall, a noted conservationist, spans over 5,600 acres of rolling mountains and protected woodlands. It offers a tranquil escape into nature with its lush forests, bubbling streams, and diverse wildlife.

One of the most striking features of Smithgall Woods State Park is Dukes Creek, which runs through the park and is celebrated as one of the premier trout fishing streams in North Georgia. The park offers carefully managed fishing days to ensure a quality experience while conserving the trout population. Anglers must apply for a special permit to fish in the creek, making for an exclusive and serene fishing experience.

Hiking is another popular activity in Smithgall Woods, with more than 23 miles of trails ranging from easy strolls to challenging treks. These trails meander through diverse habitats and offer opportunities to see wildlife such as deer, wild turkeys, and numerous bird species. The Cathy Ellis Memorial Trail is particularly noteworthy, providing educational signs that discuss the local ecology and the conservation work being done in the park.

For those interested in learning more about the natural and cultural history of the area, Smithgall Woods State Park offers a variety of programs and workshops. These include guided hikes, environmental education programs, and special events that focus on the region's wildlife and plants. The park's visitor center features exhibits on the geography and history of the area and provides resources for exploring the park.

Smithgall Woods also provides accommodations in the form of cottages that offer guests a comfortable stay amidst the natural beauty of the park. These cottages range from rustic to modern, with amenities that cater to different tastes and needs, perfect for families, couples, or solo travelers seeking a peaceful retreat.

8.   Helen Alpine Village, Helen

Helen, Georgia, is a charming re-creation of an alpine village complete with cobblestone alleys and old-world towers. This unique town, nestled in the Blue Ridge Mountains, started as a small logging community but transformed itself into a Bavarian-esque village in 1969 to promote tourism. Today, Helen is one of the most visited destinations in Georgia, known for its picturesque beauty, cultural festivals, and outdoor activities.

Walking through Helen, visitors might feel as though they've stepped into a village in the Alps. The town's architecture is styled with timber-framed houses painted in various pastels, adding to its fairy-tale ambiance. Shops, galleries, and boutiques line the streets, offering everything from handmade crafts to German food and beer.

Helen's festive atmosphere peaks during the annual Oktoberfest, the longest-running Oktoberfest in the United States. This event features German music, traditional dances, beer, and food, celebrating Helen's cultural heritage with a touch of Southern hospitality. The festivities attract visitors from all over the country, eager to enjoy a slice of Bavaria in the heart of North Georgia.

Outdoor activities abound in and around Helen. The Chattahoochee River flows through the town, providing ample opportunities for tubing, kayaking, and fishing. Nearby, the expansive Chattahoochee National Forest offers hiking trails, waterfalls, and stunning scenic views, particularly in the fall when the foliage is spectacular.

For those interested in learning more about the local culture and history, the Helen Arts & Heritage Center houses art galleries, a pottery studio, and historical exhibits. This center not only supports local artists but also serves as an educational resource for visitors.

Helen Alpine Village combines the allure of European architecture and culture with the natural beauty of the Appalachian Mountains, offering visitors a unique experience. Whether coming for the vibrant festivals, the outdoor adventures, or simply to enjoy the distinctive ambiance, Helen provides a delightful escape for all who wander through its quaint streets.

9. Unicoi State Park, Helen

Unicoi State Park, nestled in the North Georgia mountains near Helen, is a haven for adventurers and nature lovers. This 1,050-acre park provides a beautiful backdrop for a wide range of outdoor activities and offers facilities for all ages, making it a perfect destination for families, couples, and solo explorers alike.

One of the park's main attractions is Unicoi Lake, a serene 53-acre lake that invites visitors to swim, fish, and canoe in a picturesque setting. The lake is stocked with trout, making it a popular spot for fishing. Around the lake, a sandy beach and picnic areas provide perfect spots for relaxation and family gatherings.

For those looking to stay overnight, Unicoi State Park offers a variety of accommodations that range from campsites and RV sites to cozy cabins and a lodge. The lodge is particularly popular due to its comfortable amenities and beautiful views of the lake and forest. For a more secluded experience, the cabins nestled in the woods provide a peaceful retreat from the hustle and bustle of daily life.

The park's extensive trail system is a highlight for many visitors. Trails like the 7.5-mile Unicoi to Helen trail and the shorter, scenic Lake Loop Trail offer hikers of all skill levels beautiful vistas of the surrounding mountains and woodlands.

Unicoi State Park is also known for its adventurous offerings such as zip-lining and archery, catering to thrill-seekers looking to experience a bit more adrenaline. The zip-line adventures provide a unique way to view the park from above, soaring through treetops and over the lake.

Educational programs are a staple at Unicoi State Park, with year-round activities that teach visitors about local wildlife, natural history, and environmental conservation efforts.

The park's close proximity to the Alpine town of Helen allows for easy access to additional attractions and amenities, including dining, shopping, and cultural events like the annual Helen Oktoberfest. This proximity makes Unicoi State Park a convenient and desirable location for visitors looking to enjoy both outdoor activities and the charming European-inspired town of Helen.

10.   Anna Ruby Falls, Helen

Anna Ruby Falls, located near Helen in the heart of North Georgia, is a stunning natural attraction within the Chattahoochee National Forest. This rare double waterfall is formed by two creeks: the Curtis Creek and York Creek, which originate on Tray Mountain and unite at the base of the falls. The waterfalls cascade down a dramatic rocky ravine, dropping 153 feet and 50 feet respectively, into a beautiful, tranquil pool below.

Visitors to Anna Ruby Falls can access the falls via a paved half-mile trail from the parking area. This trail, known as the Anna Ruby Falls Scenic Trail, is well-maintained and relatively easy, making it accessible to most visitors, including those with mobility challenges. The path winds through a lush forested area, with informative signs that describe the local flora and fauna, making the walk both educational and enjoyable.

The viewing decks at the base of the falls provide spectacular views of both the cascading water and the surrounding forest. The sound of the water and the cool mist that rises from the falls create a refreshing and invigorating environment, perfect for photography, nature observation, or simply enjoying a moment of peace.

Anna Ruby Falls is more than just a scenic spot; it is also an area of ecological importance. The surrounding forest is home to a diverse range of plant and animal life, and the falls themselves play a crucial role in the local ecosystem. The site is a prime example of the delicate balance within mountainous watersheds and is used as an educational resource to teach visitors about environmental protection and conservation.

In addition to the natural beauty and educational value, Anna Ruby Falls offers several amenities to enhance the visitor experience, including a visitor center with exhibits on the history and ecology of the area, a gift shop, and picnic areas. The park hosts various events throughout the year, such as guided walks and environmental education programs, which add depth to the visitor experience.

11.   Sautee Nacoochee Center, Sautee Nacoochee

Sautee Nacoochee Center, located in the picturesque Sautee Nacoochee Valley near Helen, Georgia, is a cultural and historical hub dedicated to preserving and celebrating the Appalachian heritage of North Georgia. This community center is housed in a restored schoolhouse and encompasses several buildings that offer a variety of cultural and artistic programs, making it a cornerstone of the local community.

The center's main attractions include an art gallery that features rotating exhibitions from local and regional artists. These exhibitions often showcase a variety of media, including painting, sculpture, and folk art, reflecting the rich artistic traditions of the Appalachian region. The gallery not only provides a platform for artists but also offers educational opportunities for visitors to learn about the art and culture of North Georgia.

Adjacent to the gallery, the Sautee Nacoochee Center includes a performance theater that hosts a wide range of events, from live music and dance to theater and storytelling. This intimate venue is known for its excellent acoustics and welcoming atmosphere, making it a favorite among performers and audiences alike.

One of the unique aspects of the Sautee Nacoochee Center is its focus on folk traditions. The center offers classes and workshops in traditional crafts such as pottery, weaving, and woodcarving. These workshops are taught by skilled artisans and are open to people of all skill levels, from beginners to advanced practitioners. The center also hosts folk dance events and traditional music jams, preserving and promoting the cultural heritage of the Appalachian community.

The Sautee Nacoochee Center also operates a history museum that explores the rich history of the Sautee and Nacoochee Valleys. The museum features artifacts, photographs, and documents that tell the story of the area's Native American heritage, its pioneering families, and the development of the local community. The museum is an invaluable resource for anyone interested in the historical and cultural landscape of North Georgia.

12.   Toccoa Falls, Toccoa

Toccoa Falls, located on the campus of Toccoa Falls College in Toccoa, Georgia, is one of the tallest free-falling waterfalls east of the Mississippi River. This stunning natural feature, which plunges 186 feet into a serene pool below, offers a breathtaking sight that is easily accessible to visitors of all ages and abilities.

The falls are located just a short, easy walk from the college's welcome center, making them accessible even for those with limited mobility. The path leads visitors through a picturesque landscape, culminating in a viewing platform that provides unobstructed views of Toccoa Falls. The platform is an excellent spot for photography, meditation, or simply enjoying the peaceful sound of the water.

Toccoa Falls is more than just a beautiful waterfall; it is also a site of historical significance. The falls and the surrounding area have been a focal point for the local community and visitors since the 19th century. In 1977, the falls were the site of a tragic dam break that resulted in the loss of 39 lives. Today, a memorial near the falls honors those who perished in the flood, and the site serves as a reminder of the power and unpredictability of nature.

The waterfall is situated within the beautifully maintained grounds of Toccoa Falls College, which adds an element of serene beauty to the visit. The college operates a gift shop near the falls, where visitors can purchase souvenirs, snacks, and artisan goods, many of which are made by local craftsmen.

Visitors to Toccoa Falls can extend their stay by exploring other attractions in the Toccoa area, including the historic downtown, local museums, and outdoor recreational opportunities such as hiking and fishing in the nearby national forests.

Toccoa Falls offers a unique blend of natural beauty, accessibility, and historical depth, making it a must-visit destination for those traveling in Northeast Georgia. Whether you are a nature lover, a history enthusiast, or someone looking for a peaceful retreat, Toccoa Falls provides a memorable and enriching experience.

13. Tallulah Gorge State Park, Tallulah Falls

Tallulah Gorge State Park, located in the northeastern part of Georgia in Tallulah Falls, is one of the state's most dramatic natural wonders. The park encompasses Tallulah Gorge, a spectacular canyon that is two miles long and nearly 1,000 feet deep. The gorge is carved by the Tallulah River, which flows through the rugged terrain, creating a series of stunning waterfalls and rapids that attract visitors from around the world.

The park offers a variety of recreational activities that make the most of its breathtaking scenery. For those looking to explore the gorge, there are several overlooks along the rim that provide panoramic views of the canyon and the river below. For the more adventurous, a permit system allows a limited number of visitors each day to hike down to the gorge floor, where they can see the river up close and experience the raw power of the waterfalls.

One of the highlights of Tallulah Gorge State Park is the suspension bridge that sways 80 feet above the rocky floor, offering an unmatched view of the river and waterfalls. This bridge is not only a favorite spot for photography but also serves as a thrilling vantage point from which to watch kayakers navigate the challenging rapids below during scheduled whitewater release days.

For those interested in a more relaxed visit, the park offers numerous hiking and biking trails that range in difficulty and provide various perspectives of the gorge and the surrounding forest. The most popular trail, the Rim Trails, loops around the gorge, providing numerous lookouts where visitors can stop and appreciate the natural beauty of the area.

Tallulah Gorge State Park also plays an important role in conservation, protecting the unique flora and fauna of the area. The park's interpretive center offers educational exhibits about the geology of the gorge and the ecosystem's biodiversity, including rare species of plants and wildlife that thrive in this unique environment.

In addition to its natural and recreational offerings, the park hosts several events throughout the year, including guided hikes, educational programs, and spectacular aesthetic water releases in the spring and fall, which showcase the beauty of the waterfalls with dramatic flows.

14.   Lake Burton, Clayton

Nestled in the foothills of the Appalachian Mountains near Clayton, Georgia, Lake Burton is a serene and picturesque reservoir known for its clear waters and scenic beauty. Covering 2,775 acres and boasting 62 miles of shoreline, Lake Burton is the largest of the six lakes in the North Georgia chain. It's a premier destination for water sports, fishing, and lakeside living, making it a popular choice for both vacationers and permanent residents.

The lake's clear, deep waters make it ideal for a variety of water activities, including boating, water skiing, and wakeboarding. The surrounding scenery, characterized by lush forests and rolling hills, enhances the experience, providing a beautiful backdrop for water sports enthusiasts.

Anglers find Lake Burton particularly appealing because of its abundant fish populations, including spotted bass, largemouth bass, and walleye. The lake is also known for its state-record catches, which has helped build its reputation as a top fishing destination in Georgia. Several fishing tournaments are held at Lake Burton throughout the year, drawing anglers from all over the region.

For those looking to relax, the lake's numerous coves and quiet inlets provide the perfect setting for kayaking or paddleboarding. These activities offer a more peaceful way to explore the lake and enjoy its natural beauty up close.

The communities around Lake Burton are known for their hospitality and charm. The area features a range of accommodations from rustic cabins to luxurious lakeside homes. Local restaurants offer delightful dining experiences, many with views of the lake, where visitors can enjoy local cuisine after a day on the water.

Lake Burton is not only a hub for water sports and fishing but also serves as a cultural and social gathering place for the community. Seasonal events, such as the Fourth of July fireworks show and the Lake Burton Fun Run, are highlights of the year and provide opportunities for visitors and residents to come together and celebrate.

15. Chattooga River, Clayton

The Chattooga River, flowing along the border between Georgia and South Carolina, is renowned for its pristine waters, rugged scenery, and thrilling whitewater rapids. Designated as a National Wild and Scenic River, the Chattooga offers one of the premier whitewater experiences in the Eastern United States, attracting thousands of rafters, kayakers, and adventure seekers each year.

The river's untamed beauty and the challenge of its rapids are not the only draws; the Chattooga also boasts an incredible diversity of flora and fauna, making it a haven for nature enthusiasts and conservationists. The surrounding forest is lush with hardwoods and pines, and the river's banks are lined with rhododendrons and mountain laurels, providing a stunning display of color in the spring.

Whitewater rafting on the Chattooga River is divided into sections, with Section III being popular for families and beginners, offering milder rapids and plenty of opportunities to swim and enjoy the scenery. Section IV, known as the Five Falls, features some of the most intense and technical rapids on the river, providing an adrenaline-pumping ride suitable for experienced rafters.

In addition to whitewater rafting, the Chattooga River area is a prime spot for hiking, camping, and fishing. Numerous trails run along the river and through the surrounding wilderness, offering spectacular views and a chance to spot wildlife. The river itself is home to a variety of fish species, making it a popular destination for fly fishing.

The conservation efforts in the Chattooga River area have been successful in preserving its natural state, ensuring that it remains free from development and accessible only by foot. This commitment to preserving the river's wild character adds to its allure and provides a rare opportunity to experience one of the last truly wild rivers in the Southeast.

The Chattooga River's combination of natural beauty, thrilling adventure, and environmental significance makes it an exceptional destination for anyone looking to explore the great outdoors.

16.   Rabun Bald, Rabun County

Rabun Bald, with an elevation of 4,696 feet, stands as the second-highest peak in Georgia and offers some of the most stunning panoramic views in the state. Located in Rabun County, this mountain is a favored destination for hikers and nature lovers who seek the beauty and solitude of the Southern Appalachian Mountains.

The most popular route to the summit is the Rabun Bald Trail, which is accessible from the Beegum Gap trailhead. This moderately challenging hike is approximately 1.5 miles long and features a series of switchbacks through a lush, mixed hardwood forest. As hikers ascend, they pass through dense rhododendron and mountain laurel thickets, which bloom spectacularly in early summer.

The summit of Rabun Bald is marked by a unique, stone observation tower that dates back to the 1930s. This tower was originally used as a fire lookout but now serves as a perfect vantage point for visitors. From the top of the tower, hikers can enjoy a 360-degree view that encompasses four states: Georgia, North Carolina, South Carolina, and Tennessee. On clear days, the vistas are breathtaking, offering sweeping views of the Blue Ridge Mountains and beyond.

For those looking to extend their adventure, Rabun Bald is connected to a network of trails, including the Bartram Trail, which traverses a variety of terrains and offers additional scenic overlooks and access to other areas of interest within the Southern Appalachians.

Camping near Rabun Bald is also popular, with several primitive sites along the trails that offer a true wilderness experience. Nighttime on the mountain is a quiet, serene time, with star-filled skies and the sounds of nature providing a peaceful backdrop.

Rabun Bald is not only a place of natural beauty but also a site of ecological importance. The area is home to diverse wildlife, including deer, black bears, and a variety of bird species. The mountain's high elevation and relatively cool climate support plant species that are rare in other parts of Georgia, making it an important area for conservation and study.

17. Dillard House, Dillard

The Dillard House, located in the small town of Dillard, Georgia, in the picturesque North Georgia mountains, is a renowned destination that combines the charm of Southern hospitality with the beauty of the Appalachian landscape. Established in 1917 by Carrie and Arthur Dillard, the Dillard House has grown from a simple boarding house to a sprawling complex offering dining, lodging, and a variety of recreational activities, making it a beloved getaway for families, couples, and solo travelers.

The culinary experience at the Dillard House is at the heart of its appeal. Famous for its family-style Southern meals, the restaurant serves a bounty of dishes that are passed around the table, just like a family gathering. The menu changes daily but typically includes a variety of meats, vegetables, bread, and desserts, all made from fresh, local ingredients. The fried chicken, country ham, and homemade biscuits are particularly popular, and no meal is complete without trying the Dillard House's signature apple butter.

Beyond its restaurant, the Dillard House offers a range of accommodations that capture the rustic charm of its mountain setting. Guests can choose from rooms in the main inn, private cottages, and chalets that provide more space and privacy. Each option is decorated in a style that reflects the natural beauty of the surrounding area, with modern amenities to ensure a comfortable stay.

For those looking to explore the great outdoors, the Dillard House is perfectly situated. The property itself offers horseback riding, with guided trail rides that wind through scenic mountain pathways. For fishing enthusiasts, the Dillard House has trout ponds stocked with fish, providing a peaceful setting for a day of fishing. Additionally, the surrounding area is rich in natural attractions, including hiking trails, waterfalls, and the scenic vistas of the Blue Ridge Mountains.

The Dillard House also caters to events and celebrations, providing a picturesque backdrop for weddings, family reunions, and corporate retreats. The combination of excellent food, comfortable accommodations, and a stunning natural environment makes it an ideal choice for special occasions.

18.   Georgia Mountain Fairgrounds, Hiawassee

The Georgia Mountain Fairgrounds, nestled on the shores of beautiful Lake Chatuge in Hiawassee, Georgia, is far more than just a location for events; it is a cultural hub that celebrates the heritage and beauty of the North Georgia mountains. Throughout the year, the fairgrounds host a variety of events, including the famous Georgia Mountain Fair, music festivals, and arts and craft shows, drawing visitors from across the region to experience the traditions and entertainment of mountain life.

The Georgia Mountain Fair, held annually at the fairgrounds, is one of the highlights of the year and features old-fashioned fun for all ages. The fair includes musical performances, educational demonstrations, carnival rides, and delicious regional food. One of the fair's unique attractions is the Pioneer Village, a replica of a historic mountain town complete with a blacksmith shop, general store, and traditional cabins. Here, artisans demonstrate early American crafts such as pottery, quilting, and blacksmithing, offering a glimpse into the daily life of the Appalachian settlers.

Music is a significant part of the culture in the North Georgia mountains, and the Georgia Mountain Fairgrounds is known for its outstanding concerts. The Anderson Music Hall, located on the fairgrounds, hosts performances by well-known country, bluegrass, and Southern rock artists, providing top-tier entertainment in an intimate setting. The fairgrounds also host the Georgia Mountain Fall Festival, which features many musical performances, a flower show, and a fiddlers' convention.

In addition to these larger events, the fairgrounds offer facilities for camping, making it a great place to stay and enjoy the natural beauty of the area. The campgrounds are equipped with modern amenities, including hookups for RVs, laundry facilities, and easy access to Lake Chatuge, where visitors can enjoy fishing, boating, and swimming.

The Georgia Mountain Fairgrounds serves as a focal point for the community in Hiawassee and a destination for visitors seeking a taste of mountain culture and hospitality. Whether you come for a specific event, a concert, or just to enjoy a few peaceful days by the lake, the fairgrounds offer a welcoming and entertaining experience amidst the stunning scenery of North Georgia.

19. Brasstown Bald, near Hiawassee

Brasstown Bald, the highest point in Georgia, stands at an elevation of 4,784 feet and is located near Hiawassee in the North Georgia mountains. Offering breathtaking panoramic views of the surrounding states and the lush forests of the Chattahoochee-Oconee National Forest, Brasstown Bald is a must-visit for anyone exploring this scenic region.

Visitors to Brasstown Bald can reach the summit via a steep, paved 0.6-mile trail or a shuttle service that runs from the parking area to the top. At the summit, the Brasstown Bald Visitor Center and observation deck allow for unparalleled 360-degree views that on clear days can extend up to 100 miles. The visitor center also features exhibits on the geological history of the Appalachian Mountains and the cultural history of the area, as well as information about the local flora and fauna.

The area around Brasstown Bald is a haven for nature lovers and outdoor enthusiasts. Several hiking trails of varying difficulty offer more ways to explore the beauty of the highlands. These trails, including the popular Arkaquah Trail, wind through dense forests, past streams, and over rugged terrain, providing opportunities for hiking, photography, and wildlife observation.

Brasstown Bald is particularly popular in the fall when the mountain is blanketed in vibrant autumn colors. It's also a sought-after spot for stargazing and sunrise or sunset watches, thanks to its clear skies and elevated position above the surrounding landscape.

In addition to its natural attractions, Brasstown Bald plays an important role in environmental education and conservation. The site hosts a range of educational programs aimed at all ages, from school groups to adult learners, focusing on the importance of conservation and the unique ecosystems of the Appalachian highlands.

Visiting Brasstown Bald provides not only a chance to see Georgia from its highest point but also an opportunity to immerse oneself in the natural and cultural richness of the North Georgia mountains. Whether you are hiking up the mountain, learning about its history, or simply enjoying the stunning views, Brasstown Bald offers a memorable experience that highlights the beauty of this unique area.

20.   Blairsville Sorghum Festival, Blairsville

The Blairsville Sorghum Festival, held annually in Blairsville, Georgia, celebrates the art and tradition of sorghum syrup making, a practice that has deep roots in the region's agricultural history. This two-weekend event every October brings together locals and visitors to honor and enjoy this sweet syrup, which is a staple in Southern cuisine.

Sorghum syrup, made from the juice of sorghum cane, was once a common sweetener in the rural South, used in everything from baking to barbecuing. The festival not only showcases the process of making sorghum syrup—which involves harvesting the sorghum cane, pressing it to extract the juice, and then boiling the juice down into syrup—but also celebrates the broader heritage of the Appalachian region with a variety of traditional crafts, music, and foods.

The festival features live demonstrations of sorghum syrup making, offering attendees a chance to see and learn about the traditional methods used to produce it. These demonstrations are a highlight of the festival and provide a link to the agricultural practices of the past.

Apart from sorghum syrup production, the Blairsville Sorghum Festival includes a host of other activities and attractions. There are arts and crafts exhibitions, where local artisans sell handmade goods ranging from pottery to jewelry. Traditional Appalachian music is a staple of the festival, with live performances of bluegrass, country, and folk music setting a festive atmosphere.

Visitors can also participate in old-fashioned games and competitions like pole climbing, log sawing, and horseshoe pitching. For the younger crowd, there are plenty of activities designed to entertain and educate about rural life and traditions.

The festival is also famous for its food offerings, which feature dishes made with sorghum syrup and other traditional Southern ingredients. From sorghum pancakes to barbecue, the food vendors at the festival offer a delicious taste of local cuisine.

The Blairsville Sorghum Festival not only preserves the traditional craft of sorghum syrup making but also serves as a celebration of the cultural heritage of the North Georgia mountains.

21.   Southern Tree Plantation, Blairsville

Southern Tree Plantation, located in the picturesque mountains of Blairsville, Georgia, offers a unique blend of outdoor fun, agriculture, and festive events throughout the year. Spanning over a lush landscape, this family-owned and operated plantation is not just a working farm but a destination that provides a variety of activities and attractions for visitors of all ages.

One of the primary attractions of Southern Tree Plantation is its extensive Christmas tree farm. Visitors can choose and cut their own Christmas trees from a variety of species, making the experience a beloved holiday tradition for many families. The plantation grows several types of trees, ensuring that every family finds their perfect tree. During the holiday season, the farm transforms into a winter wonderland with decorations, lights, and festive music, enhancing the holiday spirit.

Beyond Christmas trees, the plantation features pumpkin patches in the fall, offering hayrides, pumpkin picking, and other autumnal activities that celebrate the season. The picturesque setting among the North Georgia mountains makes it an ideal backdrop for these seasonal festivities.

For those interested in more active pursuits, Southern Tree Plantation offers an array of outdoor recreational activities. Guests can enjoy ATV rides through the plantation's trails, petting zoo visits where children can interact with farm animals, and pony rides. The plantation also features archery ranges and areas for picnicking, making it a versatile destination for a day of fun in the outdoors.

Educational tours at the plantation teach visitors about tree farming, sustainable agriculture, and the ecology of the North Georgia mountains. These tours are designed to be informative and engaging, providing valuable insights into the operations of a working farm and the importance of conservation.

22.   Vogel State Park, Blairsville

Vogel State Park, one of Georgia's oldest and most beloved state parks, is nestled at the base of Blood Mountain in the Chattahoochee National Forest. Spanning 233 acres, this park is particularly favored for its beautiful setting in the heart of the North Georgia mountains and its proximity to the Appalachian Trail, making it a prime destination for hikers, campers, and nature lovers.

The centerpiece of Vogel State Park is Lake Trahlyta, a serene lake formed by a dam built by the Civilian Conservation Corps in the 1930s. Visitors can enjoy paddle boating and fishing in the lake or simply stroll around the scenic pathway that encircles the water. The tranquil lake, surrounded by mountains and lush forest, offers stunning views year-round, especially during the autumn months when the foliage displays vibrant colors.

Hiking is a popular activity at Vogel State Park, with trails ranging from easy walks to more challenging hikes. The 4-mile Bear Hair Gap Trail provides a moderate hike with rewarding views of the park and Lake Trahlyta from above, while the shorter Trahlyta Lake Trail offers an easy loop that is perfect for families. For a more strenuous adventure, hikers can tackle the Coosa Backcountry Trail, which offers a challenging 12.9-mile loop through rugged terrain.

Vogel State Park is also a haven for picnickers and families looking to spend a day or weekend in the great outdoors. The park features a large campground, cottages, and primitive backpacking sites, catering to a variety of outdoor experiences. Campsites are well-equipped with facilities, and many offer picturesque views of the surrounding nature.

In addition to recreational activities, Vogel State Park serves as a venue for numerous events and educational programs throughout the year, including guided hikes, wildlife presentations, and craft workshops. These programs are designed to enhance the visitor experience and provide deeper insights into the region's natural history and cultural heritage.

23. Chattahoochee-Oconee National Forests

The Chattahoochee-Oconee National Forests cover nearly 867,000 acres across the mountains and foothills of northern Georgia, offering an extensive array of natural landscapes, diverse ecosystems, and recreational activities that attract millions of visitors each year. These forests are managed as a single unit, providing some of the best outdoor recreation opportunities in the Southeast, along with crucial habitat for wildlife and a living space for a variety of plants and trees.

Visitors to the Chattahoochee-Oconee National Forests can explore over 850 miles of trails that cater to hikers, mountain bikers, and equestrians. These trails range from easy walks through scenic meadows to challenging hikes up rugged mountains, including parts of the famous Appalachian Trail. The diversity of trails ensures that visitors of all skill levels can find a route that suits their abilities and offers a chance to experience the beauty of the forest firsthand.

For water enthusiasts, the forests feature numerous rivers and lakes that provide ample opportunities for fishing, boating, and swimming. The Chattahoochee River, one of the major waterways in the forests, is popular for fishing, particularly for trout. The river's clear, cold waters make it one of the best trout fishing streams in the state. Additionally, Lake Winfield Scott and Lake Conasauga offer peaceful settings for kayaking and canoeing, surrounded by the natural beauty of the forests.

Camping is another popular activity in the Chattahoochee-Oconee National Forests, with a wide range of camping options available. From developed campgrounds with full amenities to backcountry sites that offer a more primitive and intimate experience with nature, there is something for every type of camper. These camping sites provide a great way to extend a visit to the forests and enjoy the serenity of the outdoors overnight.

Offering a blend of scenic beauty, recreational diversity, and conservation significance, the Chattahoochee-Oconee National Forests are a vital part of Georgia's natural heritage. They provide a space for people to connect with nature and enjoy the many benefits of outdoor recreation, making them a treasured resource for both the people of Georgia and visitors from around the world.

24. Blue Ridge Scenic Railway, Blue Ridge

The Blue Ridge Scenic Railway is one of the most picturesque train rides in the Southeastern United States. Starting from the charming mountain town of Blue Ridge, Georgia, this heritage railroad winds along the beautiful Toccoa River through the lush Chattahoochee National Forest to the small towns of McCaysville, Georgia, and Copperhill, Tennessee. The journey offers a leisurely way to experience the scenic beauty of the Blue Ridge Mountains while embracing the nostalgia of early-20th-century train travel.

The excursion covers a 26-mile round trip, taking approximately 4 hours, including a layover in McCaysville/Copperhill. The train consists of vintage rail cars that have been beautifully restored to reflect the era of their original use. Passengers can choose from open-air rail cars that offer unobstructed views of the surrounding landscapes and riverside vistas, or climate-controlled cars that provide comfort regardless of the weather.

The route itself is steeped in history and natural beauty. As the train chugs along the tracks, passengers are treated to views of lush forests, rolling hills, and the tranquil waters of the Toccoa River. The railway crosses several bridges, providing spectacular views and excellent opportunities for photography. During the fall, the journey becomes even more magical as the forest turns into a vibrant palette of autumn colors, making it one of the most popular times to ride the railway.

Upon reaching McCaysville/Copperhill, passengers have a layover of about two hours, allowing them to explore the twin cities, enjoy local cuisine, and shop for crafts and souvenirs. The cities are connected by a blue line that marks the state line between Georgia and Tennessee, allowing visitors to stand in two states at once, adding a unique touch to the experience.

The Blue Ridge Scenic Railway also offers special themed rides throughout the year, including holiday adventures like the Pumpkin Express and Santa Express, which are favorites among families. These themed journeys provide additional entertainment, such as storytelling, sing-alongs, and seasonal decorations, enhancing the festive atmosphere.

25. Mercier Orchards, Blue Ridge

Mercier Orchards, a family-owned and operated orchard in Blue Ridge, Georgia, is renowned for its vast array of apples and other fruits, homemade baked goods, and a variety of agricultural products. Established in 1943, Mercier Orchards is one of the largest apple orchards in the Southeast and a staple of the community, offering a rich agricultural experience for visitors year-round.

Spanning over 300 acres, the orchard grows a wide variety of fruits, including apples, peaches, cherries, blueberries, and strawberries, depending on the season. Visitors to Mercier Orchards can participate in "U-Pick" events, a family-friendly activity that allows them to pick their own fruit directly from the trees and bushes. This hands-on experience is particularly popular among families and provides a fun and educational way to learn about where food comes from and how it grows.

In addition to fruit picking, Mercier Orchards is famous for its farm market, which sells a wide range of products produced on-site. The market features freshly baked pies, homemade jellies, and apple cider donuts that are a must-try for anyone visiting the orchard. The orchard also produces its own hard cider and wines, with a tasting room where visitors can sample and purchase these adult beverages crafted from the orchard's own fruits.

Mercier Orchards hosts a variety of events throughout the year, including seasonal festivals, cooking classes, and educational tours. These events often feature live music, food tastings, and workshops that highlight the orchard's produce and products.

One of the most cherished times to visit Mercier Orchards is during the autumn months when the orchard hosts its annual Apple Festival. During this festival, the orchard celebrates the apple harvest with a weekend full of activities, including hayrides, a corn maze, apple cannon shootings, and more. This festive atmosphere, combined with the stunning fall foliage of the surrounding mountains, makes it a perfect family outing.

Mercier Orchards is more than just a place to buy apples; it's a destination that offers a glimpse into the life of North Georgia's agricultural community.

Central and Eastern Georgia

1. **Phinizy Swamp Nature Park, Augusta**

Phinizy Swamp Nature Park in Augusta, Georgia, offers a tranquil escape into nature with its lush wetlands and diverse ecosystems. Spanning over 1,100 acres, this park is a research and education center that provides visitors with the opportunity to learn about wetland ecology while enjoying the serene beauty of its landscapes.

The park features a network of boardwalks and trails that wind through forests and wetlands, allowing visitors to explore without disturbing the delicate habitats. These trails are perfect for bird watching, as the park is home to a variety of bird species, including herons, egrets, and the occasional bald eagle. The observation decks along the trails provide excellent vantage points for wildlife observation and photography.

Phinizy Swamp Nature Park is also a center for environmental research and education. The park's visitor center offers educational exhibits that explain the functions and values of wetlands, including their role in water purification and flood control. These exhibits are designed to be informative for all ages, making the park a valuable resource for school groups and families.

Regularly scheduled guided tours and educational programs are available, offering deeper insights into the park's natural and scientific significance. These programs cover topics such as wildlife habitats, conservation efforts, and the importance of wetlands to the environment and human communities.

For those who prefer a more leisurely visit, the park offers plenty of spots for picnicking and relaxing. The natural scenery and quiet atmosphere make it an ideal place for contemplation and rejuvenation. Phinizy Swamp Nature Park also hosts special events throughout the year, including night hikes, photography workshops, and birding walks, which take advantage of the park's rich natural resources and scenic beauty.

2. Augusta Canal Discovery Center, Augusta

Located in the historic Enterprise Mill, the Augusta Canal Discovery Center serves as a gateway to understanding Augusta's pivotal role in the industrial history of Georgia. The center offers interactive exhibits and educational displays that chronicle the construction and impact of the Augusta Canal, one of the only intact American canal systems with continuous water flow.

Visitors to the Discovery Center can explore the history of the canal through engaging multimedia presentations and artifacts that illustrate how the canal was used to harness the Savannah River's power for manufacturing and transportation during the Civil War and beyond. The exhibits also detail how the canal influenced the development of Augusta, transforming it into a powerhouse of textile manufacturing in the South.

One of the highlights of visiting the Augusta Canal Discovery Center is taking a guided boat tour along the canal itself. These tours provide a unique perspective on the area's history and natural beauty, floating past several historic mill buildings and under picturesque old bridges. The tours also offer a chance to see local wildlife, including birds, turtles, and occasionally otters.

The Discovery Center is also the starting point for several recreational activities along the canal's towpath. Visitors can rent bicycles or bring their own to explore the scenic multi-use trail that follows the canal's banks. The path is popular among joggers, cyclists, and walkers who enjoy the blend of historic architecture, urban green space, and natural scenery.

For educators and students, the Augusta Canal Discovery Center offers tailored educational programs that align with state curriculum standards. These programs emphasize STEM concepts and provide hands-on learning opportunities about water management, renewable energy, and industrial history.

The Augusta Canal Discovery Center not only educates about Augusta's past but also celebrates the canal's role in the city's present and future. It remains an important site for understanding the industrial heritage of the South and serves as a centerpiece for recreation and conservation efforts in Augusta today.

3. Morris Museum of Art, Augusta

The Morris Museum of Art in Augusta is the first museum dedicated to the art and artists of the American South. Located on the Riverwalk in the heart of downtown Augusta, the museum houses a remarkable collection of nearly 5,000 works of art, ranging from traditional to contemporary styles, reflecting the rich cultural heritage of the Southern United States.

The museum's permanent collection includes an impressive array of paintings, sculptures, and works on paper that date from the late-eighteenth century to the present. Notable works include pieces by celebrated artists such as Walton Ford, William Christenberry, and Bo Bartlett. The collection emphasizes themes central to the Southern experience, including the landscape, people, history, and the cultural evolution of the South.

In addition to its permanent exhibits, the Morris Museum of Art hosts temporary exhibitions that explore significant aspects of Southern art and culture. These exhibits often feature contemporary Southern artists, providing a platform for emerging talents and modern perspectives on Southern life. The museum also offers a variety of educational programs, artist talks, and workshops that engage the community and enhance visitors' understanding of art and culture.

The museum's educational outreach extends to all ages, with programs designed specifically for children and families, including storytelling sessions, art-making activities, and guided tours. These programs aim to inspire creativity and appreciation for the arts in the young minds of visitors.

The Morris Museum of Art also plays a pivotal role in Augusta's cultural scene by hosting events such as music performances, film screenings, and literary readings that celebrate the arts in the South. These events often draw on the themes of the museum's exhibits, creating a multidimensional cultural experience.

4.   Riverwalk Augusta, Augusta

Riverwalk Augusta is a scenic urban park that stretches along the banks of the Savannah River in downtown Augusta, Georgia. This beloved green space offers a peaceful escape from the urban environment and provides locals and visitors alike a beautiful setting for relaxation, recreation, and entertainment.

The Riverwalk features two levels of brick-lined walkways, lush gardens, and spacious lawns that invite leisurely strolls, picnics, and outdoor gatherings. Along the walk, visitors can enjoy various sculptures and artworks, as well as memorials that pay homage to Augusta's historical and cultural significance. The park's benches and swings facing the river offer serene spots to relax and watch boats glide by.

One of the main attractions along the Riverwalk is the Jessye Norman Amphitheater, named after the famed opera singer and Augusta native. This open-air venue hosts concerts, festivals, and community events throughout the year, adding to the lively atmosphere of the Riverwalk. Nearby, the Saturday Market features local artisans, farmers, and food vendors, making it a popular destination for those looking to sample local produce and crafts.

The Riverwalk also serves as a link to several other attractions in downtown Augusta. It provides direct access to the Augusta Canal Discovery Center, the Morris Museum of Art, and the historic downtown area, making it a central component in exploring Augusta's charm.

Fitness enthusiasts will find the Riverwalk ideal for jogging, cycling, and other outdoor activities. The flat, well-maintained paths, combined with the scenic river and city views, make exercising an enjoyable experience. Families with children can appreciate the playgrounds and open spaces, which provide ample room for kids to play.

Riverwalk Augusta is not just a pathway along the river; it is a vibrant part of the community that offers a blend of natural beauty, recreational facilities, and cultural attractions. Whether you are looking for a place to relax, a venue to enjoy live music, or a picturesque setting for a leisurely walk, Riverwalk Augusta is a must-visit destination in the heart of the city.

5. Augusta National Golf Club (home of The Masters)

Augusta National Golf Club in Augusta, Georgia, is one of the most revered and exclusive golf clubs in the world, known primarily for hosting The Masters Tournament every spring. This invitational professional golf tournament is one of the four major championships in men's professional golf, and it is famous for its tradition, beauty, and the elite level of competition it attracts.

Founded by Bobby Jones and Clifford Roberts, Augusta National opened in 1933 and has been the stage for some of golf's most memorable moments. The course itself, designed by Jones and Alister MacKenzie, is renowned for its immaculate condition, challenging holes, and stunning beauty. Each hole is named after a plant or shrub that is prevalent on the site, such as "Magnolia," "Azalea," and "Dogwood," adding to the unique character and tradition of the course.

Augusta National is famous for its pristine fairways, strategically placed bunkers, and fast, undulating greens that challenge even the most skilled golfers. The layout demands precision and strategy, with each hole presenting a different challenge. The course has undergone several modifications over the years to keep up with advances in equipment and changes in playing style, ensuring that it remains a rigorous test of golf.

Visiting Augusta National is an exclusive experience, as the club maintains strict privacy and the course is not open to the public. However, during The Masters, spectators from around the world flock to Augusta to watch the tournament, making it one of the most attended golf events globally. The atmosphere during The Masters is electric, filled with tradition and anticipation, as patrons experience the beauty of the course in full bloom and witness the top golfers compete at the highest level.

In addition to The Masters, Augusta National is steeped in rich history and tradition. The club adheres to many long-standing traditions, such as the Champions Dinner, the Green Jacket, and the honorary tee shots at the opening of the tournament. The club's exclusive membership has included some of the most influential figures in golf and public life, adding to its mystique and allure.

6.   Elijah Clark State Park, Lincolnton

Elijah Clark State Park, located on the western shore of Clarks Hill Lake near Lincolnton, Georgia, is a haven for outdoor enthusiasts and history buffs alike. Named after a frontiersman and Revolutionary War hero, the park spans over 400 acres and offers a variety of recreational activities set against the backdrop of Georgia's natural beauty.

The park's centerpiece, Clarks Hill Lake, provides ample opportunities for water-based recreation. With over 70,000 acres of fresh water, visitors can enjoy boating, fishing, and water skiing in one of Georgia's largest lakes. The lake is known for its excellent bass fishing, and several fishing tournaments are held here annually. For those without their own boat, the park offers boat rentals, including kayaks and canoes, allowing everyone to take advantage of the water.

Elijah Clark State Park is also a great destination for camping, with more than 160 campsites ranging from full-hookup sites for RVs to primitive tent sites nestled in the woods. Each site offers easy access to the lake, providing a peaceful setting for an overnight stay under the stars. For visitors looking for comfort, the park also features fully equipped cottages that overlook the lake, offering beautiful views and a bit more privacy.

Hiking enthusiasts will find several miles of trails that meander through the park, offering picturesque views of the lake and surrounding forest. These trails are perfect for a leisurely walk or a more strenuous hike, with plenty of opportunities to observe local wildlife and enjoy the serene natural environment.

The park's historic component includes a replica of the log cabin home of Elijah Clark, furnished with artifacts from the 18th century to provide a glimpse into the life of Georgia's colonial settlers. This historical site offers educational programs and demonstrations, particularly during special events and holidays, bringing history to life for visitors of all ages.

7. Washington-Wilkes Historical Museum, Washington

The Washington-Wilkes Historical Museum, located in the charming town of Washington, Georgia, is dedicated to preserving and showcasing the rich history of Washington and the surrounding Wilkes County. Housed in a historic 1835 home, the museum offers a deep dive into the area's past, from its early days as a frontier settlement to its pivotal role in the Civil War and beyond.

The museum's extensive collection includes a variety of artifacts, photographs, documents, and exhibits that tell the story of the region. Visitors can explore exhibits that cover the Revolutionary War, the Civil War, the area's involvement in the cotton industry, and the everyday lives of the people who lived here through different eras. One of the highlights is the collection of Civil War relics, which includes weapons, uniforms, and personal items from soldiers who fought in the war.

One of the museum's unique features is its focus on the architectural heritage of the area. It includes detailed models and photographs of historic homes and buildings, many of which are still standing and part of local tours. This focus helps visitors understand the architectural styles prevalent in the South during the 18th and 19th centuries and the importance of preservation efforts.

The Washington-Wilkes Historical Museum is not just a repository of artifacts; it is a center for education and community engagement. It hosts a variety of events throughout the year, including lectures, workshops, and historical reenactments that bring history to life for people of all ages. These events provide context to the museum's exhibits and highlight the ongoing relevance of historical study.

For history enthusiasts and those interested in the cultural heritage of Georgia, the Washington-Wilkes Historical Museum offers a comprehensive and engaging overview of a town and county that have played significant roles in the state's history. Visiting the museum provides a deeper appreciation for the events that have shaped the region and the efforts to preserve its rich history for future generations.

8.   A.H. Stephens State Park, Crawfordville

A.H. Stephens State Park, located in Crawfordville, Georgia, offers visitors a mix of historical significance and recreational activities. Named after Alexander Hamilton Stephens, the vice president of the Confederacy and later Governor of Georgia, the park is part historical site and part recreational area, providing a multifaceted visitor experience.

The park's historical component is centered around the restored A.H. Stephens home, also known as Liberty Hall. The home is furnished with 19th-century artifacts and offers guided tours that provide insights into Stephens' life and times. The site also features a museum that houses one of the largest collections of Civil War artifacts in Georgia, including documents, photographs, and personal belongings of Stephens.

In addition to its historical offerings, A.H. Stephens State Park is also a destination for outdoor recreation. The park features over 1,177 acres of beautiful wooded areas and open spaces, perfect for a variety of activities. Hikers can explore more than 12 miles of trails that wind through the forest and around the park's scenic lake. The trails are well-maintained and suitable for all skill levels.

For those interested in equestrian activities, the park has a full-service horseback riding facility, including a stable, riding trails, and overnight campsites designed specifically for horse owners. The equestrian trails offer a unique way to experience the park's natural beauty, traversing through diverse landscapes and offering chances to spot wildlife.

The park also includes a 22-acre lake that invites fishing and boating. The lake is stocked with bass, bream, and catfish, making it a popular spot for anglers. Rowboats and pedal boats are available for rent, allowing everyone to enjoy time on the water.

Camping is another popular activity at A.H. Stephens State Park, with facilities that cater to both tents and RVs. The campsites are well-equipped and provide a great base from which to explore the park and the surrounding area.

9.   Lake Oconee, Greensboro

Lake Oconee, nestled in the heart of Georgia's lake country near Greensboro, is a prime destination for those seeking both relaxation and adventure. As the state's second-largest lake, it spans 19,000 acres and stretches over 374 miles of shoreline, offering a picturesque setting for a variety of recreational activities and leisurely pursuits.

The lake is renowned for its exceptional conditions for fishing, boasting a rich population of bass, crappie, catfish, and bream. Anglers of all skill levels find the lake a year-round fishing haven, with numerous fishing tournaments held here, drawing enthusiasts from across the region. The clear waters and abundant fish make Lake Oconee a fisherman's paradise.

Boating is another popular activity on Lake Oconee. With its vast expanse and scenic beauty, the lake is ideal for all types of watercraft, from speedboats and pontoons to kayaks and paddleboards. Several marinas around the lake provide boat rentals, supplies, and docking facilities, making it easy for visitors to get out on the water and enjoy the serene environment.

For those looking to relax on the shores, Lake Oconee offers a multitude of options for waterfront lodging, ranging from luxury resorts to cozy lakeside cabins. The Ritz-Carlton Reynolds, Lake Oconee, is one of the most prestigious accommodations, providing guests with upscale amenities, a world-class golf course, and spa services, all set against the backdrop of the lake's tranquil waters.

Lake Oconee is not just a hub of water-based activities; it is also surrounded by a landscape rich in beauty and opportunities for adventure. The area features several golf courses known for their beautiful lake views and challenging holes, making it a popular destination for golf enthusiasts. Hiking and biking trails around the lake offer another way to explore the natural beauty of the area, with paths winding through lush forests and along the water's edge.

The lake also serves as a venue for a variety of events throughout the year, including music festivals, craft fairs, and culinary events, which utilize the picturesque setting to enhance the experience. These events provide a taste of local culture and hospitality, making Lake Oconee a vibrant community as well as a recreational hub.

10. Rock Eagle 4-H Center, Eatonton

Located in Eatonton, Georgia, the Rock Eagle 4-H Center is more than just a camp; it is a hub for youth development, environmental education, and community engagement. Spanning 1,500 acres, the center is named after its most famous feature: an ancient rock mound in the shape of an eagle. This prehistoric effigy mound, believed to be over 2,000 years old, is a significant archaeological site and a poignant reminder of the area's rich Native American heritage.

Rock Eagle 4-H Center serves as a premier site for the University of Georgia's Cooperative Extension 4-H program, offering a wide range of educational programs and camps that focus on agriculture, environmental science, leadership, and more. These programs are designed to foster development and provide young people with the skills and knowledge to become future leaders and responsible citizens.

The center's facilities include modern lodges, a large dining hall, conference centers, and outdoor classrooms, making it well-equipped to host educational programs, workshops, and conferences. The extensive grounds feature several nature trails, a lake for canoeing and fishing, and outdoor pavilions, allowing visitors to learn about and engage with the natural environment.

One of the unique aspects of Rock Eagle 4-H Center is its focus on environmental education. The center offers a variety of hands-on learning experiences, such as wildlife studies, forest ecology, and conservation projects, which are integrated into the camp and school programs. These initiatives are aimed at promoting environmental stewardship and teaching young people about the importance of sustainable practices.

In addition to its educational and recreational activities, Rock Eagle 4-H Center hosts special events throughout the year, including environmental education days, family weekends, and cultural festivals. These events often incorporate the center's natural and archaeological features, providing enriching experiences that connect participants with the history and ecology of the region.

11.   Madison Historic District, Madison

Madison Historic District in Madison, Georgia, stands as one of the state's most picturesque and well-preserved antebellum districts. Known for its rich history and stunning architecture, Madison has often been called "The Town Sherman Refused to Burn" during his infamous March to the Sea in the Civil War. This moniker references the legend that the town's beauty spared it from destruction, leaving its historic core largely intact to this day.

The district is home to over 100 antebellum structures and several post-Civil War buildings, showcasing a range of architectural styles, including Greek Revival, Gothic Revival, and Federal. This architectural diversity provides a tangible link to the past and offers an immersive experience for those interested in the Southern heritage and history.

Walking tours of the Madison Historic District are a popular way to explore the area, with visitors able to stroll along tree-lined streets, past beautifully restored homes, and into public buildings that have stood the test of time. The Heritage Hall, a stunning 1811 home, and the Madison-Morgan Cultural Center, a restored 1895 Romanesque Revival building, are highlights of these tours, offering insights into the lifestyle and culture of the South during the 19th century.

Madison also hosts several cultural events and festivals that celebrate its historical and architectural significance. These include the Madison Antiques Show and Sale, the Tour of Homes during Christmas, and various garden clubs' events, which attract visitors from across the region and contribute to the town's vibrant community life.

For history buffs and architecture enthusiasts, Madison Historic District offers a profound connection to Georgia's antebellum past, while its active preservation efforts and community engagement ensure that this heritage will continue to be appreciated for generations to come.

12. The State Botanical Garden of Georgia, Athens

The State Botanical Garden of Georgia, located in Athens, is a magnificent 313-acre preserve that serves as both a conservation center and a place of beauty. Managed by the University of Georgia, it is dedicated to the study and promotion of the flora of Georgia and beyond, providing a rich resource for students, researchers, and the general public.

The garden features a variety of themed gardens and collections that showcase different ecological regions and horticultural practices. These include the Flower Garden, which displays both native and exotic plants arranged in stunning designs; the Heritage Garden, which focuses on plants significant to Georgia's history; and the International Garden, which highlights the global connections of various plant species.

The garden is also renowned for its impressive conservatory, which houses tropical and subtropical plants from around the world. This facility allows visitors to experience a diverse range of flora, regardless of the outdoor weather conditions, making it a year-round destination for plant lovers.

Beyond its role as a showcase for plant diversity, the State Botanical Garden of Georgia is heavily involved in conservation efforts. It operates several programs aimed at preserving Georgia's native plant species, including habitat restoration projects and a rare plant propagation program. These efforts are vital in maintaining the state's biodiversity and educating the public about the importance of ecological stewardship.

The garden also offers a wide range of educational programs, workshops, and events designed to engage the public and provide deeper insights into the world of botany and horticulture. These include classes on garden design, botanical illustration, and plant conservation, as well as guided tours and children's activities that make the garden a dynamic place for learning and discovery.

13.   Georgia Museum of Art, Athens

The Georgia Museum of Art, located on the University of Georgia campus in Athens, serves as both the official state museum of art and an academic museum, enriching the cultural and educational landscape of the region. Opened in 1948 and accredited by the American Alliance of Museums, this vibrant institution offers a window into the world of art through its extensive collections, exhibitions, and programs.

The museum's collection includes over 12,000 works, encompassing a wide range of art forms and eras, with particular strengths in American painting, European prints, and decorative arts. Notable for its collection of American art from the nineteenth and twentieth centuries, the museum also houses significant works from renowned artists such as Georgia O'Keeffe, Winslow Homer, and Andrew Wyeth. Additionally, it features an expanding collection of works from Southern artists, reflecting its geographical roots and commitment to regional culture.

One of the standout features of the Georgia Museum of Art is its dynamic program of temporary exhibitions. These exhibitions often explore themes of historical and contemporary significance, ranging from classical to modern art, and feature works from around the world. This program not only enhances the museum's educational role but also enriches the cultural offerings available to the public.

The museum is also deeply committed to educational outreach, offering a wide array of programs designed to engage different audiences. These include lectures, symposia, workshops, and family days that provide interactive learning experiences related to current exhibitions and collections. For students and researchers, the museum offers unique opportunities for academic enhancement and professional development through internships, fellowships, and access to its extensive research library.

Facilities at the museum include a well-appointed auditorium, a café, and a gift shop, making it a welcoming place for visitors to enjoy art in a comfortable and supportive environment. The museum's elegant sculpture garden provides a tranquil outdoor space where visitors can enjoy art in a natural setting, adding another dimension to the museum experience.

14.   University of Georgia Campus, Athens

Founded in 1785 as the country's first state-chartered university, UGA's campus is a vibrant mix of historical architecture, expansive green spaces, and state-of-the-art facilities, reflecting its long history and commitment to innovation in higher education.

Spanning over 762 acres in the heart of Athens, the campus is known for its iconic North Campus. This area features beautiful antebellum architecture, like the Chapel and the Old College, both of which are among the oldest buildings on campus. The North Campus is also home to the historic Herty Field, where the first UGA football games were played, now a tranquil green space for students and visitors alike.

The University of Georgia is also famous for its horticultural beauty, evidenced by its designation as an arboretum. Walking through the campus, visitors can enjoy an array of botanical gardens and meticulously maintained landscapes that highlight both native and exotic plant species. The Founders Memorial Garden, a small formal garden commemorating the university's founders, is a particularly serene spot that attracts visitors year-round.

For those interested in the arts, the Lamar Dodd School of Art offers galleries featuring works by students, faculty, and visiting artists, enriching the campus's cultural offerings. The Performing Arts Center, another key feature of the campus, hosts performances ranging from concerts and ballets to Broadway shows, providing high-quality entertainment for both the university and the wider community.

Athletics are a central part of the campus experience at UGA, home to the Georgia Bulldogs. The Sanford Stadium, one of the country's largest university football stadiums, is a hub of activity during the football season, filled with the spirit and traditions that embody college sports.

Educational tours of the campus are available, offering insights into its rich history, architectural heritage, and academic life. These tours provide a deeper understanding of how the university has evolved over its more than two centuries of existence and its current role as a leader in education, research, and public service.

15. The Georgia Theatre, Athens

The Georgia Theatre, a prominent music venue in downtown Athens, Georgia, holds a storied place in the American music scene. Originally built in the 1880s as a YMCA, it was transformed into a music venue in the late 1970s and has since become a crucible of musical innovation, particularly influential in the alternative music movement of the 1980s and 1990s.

This iconic venue has hosted a wide array of performances, from local emerging artists to internationally renowned bands. It is particularly noted for its role in the rise of famous bands such as R.E.M. and the B-52s, who performed there during their early years. Today, the Georgia Theatre continues to be a pivotal platform for both new and established artists, spanning a diverse range of genres.

The theatre's interior, with its multi-level layout and open-floor design, creates an intimate concert experience, allowing audiences to feel a close connection with the performers. The venue underwent significant renovations after a fire in 2009, which modernized its facilities while preserving its historic charm. It now features state-of-the-art sound and lighting systems, enhancing the quality of performances and the overall spectator experience.

In addition to its main concert hall, the Georgia Theatre includes a rooftop restaurant and bar, offering views of downtown Athens and an ideal spot for pre-concert meals or after-show drinks. This space is not only a place to enjoy food and drinks but also hosts smaller musical acts and private events, adding to the venue's dynamic use.

The Georgia Theatre is more than a concert venue; it is a cultural institution in Athens, deeply intertwined with the city's identity as a music capital. The theatre also engages in community outreach, participating in local festivals and arts education programs, which strengthens its ties with the community and supports the local arts scene.

For music lovers and cultural tourists, a visit to the Georgia Theatre offers a chance to experience live performances in a venue that has played a significant role in American music history. It remains a symbol of Athens' vibrant cultural life and a must-visit destination for anyone seeking to immerse themselves in the local music and arts scene.

16.   Sandy Creek Nature Center, Athens

Sandy Creek Nature Center is a vital educational and recreational resource located in Athens, Georgia. Spanning over 225 acres, this expansive facility is dedicated to promoting environmental awareness and conservation through its interactive exhibits, diverse wildlife habitats, and extensive network of trails.

The center features a state-of-the-art facility, the Education and Visitor Center, which houses interactive exhibits on local flora and fauna, as well as the ecology of Georgia. These exhibits provide visitors of all ages with a hands-on learning experience, enhancing their understanding of environmental issues and the natural world. The center also serves as a hub for a variety of educational programs, including workshops, guided hikes, and wildlife observation activities, all designed to foster a deeper connection with nature.

Outside, Sandy Creek Nature Center offers more than four miles of trails that meander through diverse ecosystems, including wetlands, forests, and along Sandy Creek itself. These trails offer excellent opportunities for hiking, bird watching, and encountering wildlife in their natural habitats. The trails are well-maintained and vary in difficulty to accommodate both casual visitors and more serious hikers looking to explore the natural beauty of the area.

One of the unique features of Sandy Creek Nature Center is its commitment to sustainability and conservation. The center incorporates green technologies and sustainable practices in its operations and maintenance, serving as a model for environmental stewardship. Additionally, the center participates in local conservation efforts, including habitat restoration projects and wildlife protection initiatives, playing an active role in preserving the local environment.

The nature center also hosts seasonal events and programs that celebrate the natural world, such as Earth Day festivals, night walks, and astronomy evenings, which are popular with families and school groups. These events not only provide fun and education but also highlight the center's role as a community resource for environmental education and awareness.

17. Watson Mill Bridge State Park, Comer

Watson Mill Bridge State Park, located in Comer, Georgia, is not only notable for its natural beauty but also for housing one of the longest covered bridges in the state. Spanning 229 feet across the South Fork River, the bridge, built in the early 20th century, is a splendid example of classical wooden bridge construction and a centerpiece of the park's scenic landscape.

The park extends over 1,018 acres and offers a diverse range of outdoor activities set against the backdrop of Georgia's rolling countryside. Hiking and equestrian trails wind through the park, offering various lengths and difficulties that cater to all types of visitors, from casual walkers to more serious horseback riders looking to explore deeper into the natural terrain.

One of the primary attractions of Watson Mill Bridge State Park is its extensive network of trails. Over 14 miles of trails are dedicated to equestrian use, and about 3 miles are set aside for hiking. These trails not only provide excellent opportunities for physical activity but also offer the chance to observe local wildlife and the lush vegetation of the region.

For water enthusiasts, the river provides opportunities for kayaking, canoeing, and fishing. The gentle flow of the South Fork River makes it an excellent spot for families or beginners to enjoy a day on the water. Anglers will find a healthy population of redbreast sunfish, largemouth bass, and catfish.

The park also includes a campground with over 20 sites available for tents and RVs, offering visitors the chance to stay overnight and enjoy the starlit rural sky. Each campsite is equipped with the necessary amenities to ensure a comfortable stay, including picnic tables, grills, and access to water and electricity.

Educational programs are a staple at Watson Mill Bridge State Park, with offerings that educate visitors about the local ecosystem, the history of the area, and the architecture of the covered bridge itself. These programs are designed to enhance the visitor experience and foster a deeper appreciation for Georgia's natural and historical heritage.

18.   Fort Yargo State Park, Winder

Fort Yargo State Park, nestled between Atlanta and Athens in Winder, Georgia, offers a variety of recreational activities and historical significance, making it a popular destination for families, adventure seekers, and history enthusiasts. This 1,816-acre park features a 260-acre lake, a historic fort built in 1792, and more than 20 miles of trails.

The park's centerpiece, Fort Yargo, offers a glimpse into the late 18th-century frontier life. The fort, originally constructed as a defense against Creek and Cherokee tribes, is one of the few remaining structures of its kind in Georgia and provides educational insights through guided tours and scheduled historical reenactments.

The large lake at Fort Yargo invites visitors to engage in numerous water activities such as fishing, swimming, and boating. With a well-maintained beach area and boat rental facilities available, the lake is perfect for a summer day's escape. Anglers can enjoy catching bass, catfish, and crappie, either from the shore or a boat.

For those who prefer land-based activities, the park offers a wide array of options. Over 20 miles of multi-use trails cater to hikers, mountain bikers, and runners, offering easy to challenging paths that meander through the forested park. The Mountain Bike Trail, a particular favorite, provides a thrilling ride with its series of jumps and elevation changes.

Camping at Fort Yargo is also a major draw, with facilities that cater to both tents and RVs. Additionally, yurts and cottages provide comfortable accommodations for those who prefer a more home-like setting within the natural surroundings.

Fort Yargo State Park is not only a haven for recreational activities but also a venue for various events throughout the year, including adventure races, family fishing days, and educational workshops. These events, combined with the park's natural and historical features, make it a comprehensive destination for visitors looking to explore Georgia's rich history and enjoy its natural beauty.

19.   The Allman Brothers Band Museum at The Big House

The Allman Brothers Band Museum, also known as The Big House, is located in Macon, Georgia, and serves as a tribute to one of the most influential rock bands of the 1970s. The museum is housed in the actual residence where members of the band, their families, and friends lived between 1970 and 1973, a period of intense creativity and success for the group.

The Big House has been meticulously restored and converted into a museum that offers fans and history buffs alike a deeply immersive experience into the life and times of The Allman Brothers Band. The museum showcases an extensive array of memorabilia, including original instruments, stage outfits, personal photographs, and handwritten lyrics.

Visitors to the museum can explore the rooms where the band members wrote songs and rehearsed, including the iconic "Casbah Room" that features original decor from the era. Each room in the house tells a different part of the band's story, from their meteoric rise to fame to the challenges they faced along the way.

One of the highlights of the museum is the vast collection of archival material that provides insight into the band's musical influences and the development of Southern rock. Audio guides and documentary films are available to enhance the visitor experience, offering intimate anecdotes and music clips that bring the band's history to life.

The Allman Brothers Band Museum is more than just a collection of artifacts; it is a cultural center that hosts music events, including concerts and jam sessions, which celebrate the legacy of the Allman Brothers Band and its contribution to American music. These events often feature musicians who continue to be inspired by the band's work.

For fans of The Allman Brothers Band and music historians, The Big House offers a unique journey into a pivotal moment in rock history. It stands as a testament to the band's enduring influence and is a must-visit for anyone interested in the roots of rock and roll.

20. Rose Hill Cemetery, Macon

Rose Hill Cemetery, established in 1840, is not only one of Macon, Georgia's most significant historical sites but also a tranquil place of beauty. Located on the banks of the Ocmulgee River, the cemetery spans over 70 acres and is the final resting place for many of Georgia's notable historical figures, including soldiers, politicians, and artists.

The cemetery is perhaps best known for being the burial site of members of The Allman Brothers Band, including Duane Allman and Berry Oakley. Their graves have become a pilgrimage site for fans, adorned with guitar picks, flowers, and personal notes, reflecting the deep connection between the band and their audience.

Rose Hill Cemetery is distinguished by its rolling hills, ancient oaks, and meticulously designed landscapes, which make it a peaceful place for reflection. The Victorian and Gothic revival monuments, elaborate mausoleums, and statues add to its historic and artistic appeal, making it a significant example of 19th-century cemetery architecture.

Guided tours are available, offering insights into the lives of those interred here, as well as the symbolic meanings behind the various sculptures and mausoleums. These tours highlight the cemetery's importance as a cultural and historical record of Macon's past.

In addition to its role as a traditional cemetery, Rose Hill is a venue for historical reenactments, theatrical performances, and walking tours that bring to life the rich history of Macon. These events provide a deeper understanding of the historical context surrounding the figures buried here and their contributions to Georgia's history.

As a place of eternal rest for Macon's historical figures and a site of beauty and tranquility, Rose Hill Cemetery offers visitors a unique glimpse into the past and a quiet space to appreciate the intertwining of nature, art, and history.

21.   Georgia Sports Hall of Fame, Macon

Located in the heart of Macon, Georgia, the Georgia Sports Hall of Fame stands as the largest state sports museum in the United States. Spanning over 43,000 square feet, this museum is dedicated to celebrating the achievements of Georgia's athletes, coaches, and sports figures who have made significant contributions to sports across all levels.

The museum's expansive space is filled with exhibits and memorabilia that capture the spirit of competition and highlight the rich sports heritage of Georgia. The Hall of Fame features a diverse array of sports, including football, baseball, basketball, Olympic sports, and more, ensuring that there is something to capture the interest of every sports fan.

Visitors are greeted with interactive displays and engaging exhibits that detail the lives and careers of inductees. These include legendary figures such as Hank Aaron, Bobby Jones, and Herschel Walker, among others. The museum does an excellent job of telling their stories through personal artifacts, video highlights, and immersive displays that allow visitors to experience the thrill of the game and the dedication required at the highest levels of athletic achievement.

One of the highlights of the Georgia Sports Hall of Fame is the Hall of Fame corridor, where the inductees are honored with plaques that bear their names and achievements. This corridor serves as a walk through the history of sports in Georgia, celebrating those who have excelled in their respective fields.

The museum also serves as an educational resource, offering programs and events designed to inspire the next generation of athletes and sports enthusiasts. These programs often include sports clinics, guest speakers, and interactive workshops that focus on the values of teamwork, perseverance, and sportsmanship.

Additionally, the museum hosts special exhibitions and temporary displays that focus on specific aspects of sports history or highlight current sports trends and achievements. These exhibitions provide fresh content and perspectives, making each visit unique.

22.   Tubman Museum, Macon

The Tubman Museum, located in Macon, Georgia, is the largest museum in the Southeast dedicated to educating people about the art, history, and culture of African Americans. Named after Harriet Tubman, the renowned abolitionist and humanitarian, the museum has been an integral part of Macon's cultural landscape since its founding in 1981.

Spanning an impressive 49,000 square feet, the Tubman Museum's exhibits and programs offer a comprehensive exploration of African American history, from slavery and the Civil Rights movement to contemporary art and cultural expressions. The museum's permanent exhibits include "From Africa to America," which traces the journey of African Americans from their ancestral homelands to the present day in the United States.

One of the museum's most striking features is the "Murals of the Journey," a series of large-scale murals that depict pivotal moments in African American history. These artworks are both educational and moving, providing visual narratives that enhance visitors' understanding of the struggles and triumphs of African Americans through the centuries.

The museum also houses a significant collection of African American art, showcasing works from both well-known and emerging artists. This collection highlights the rich artistic tradition within the African American community and its vital role in the broader narrative of American art.

Educational programs at the Tubman Museum are designed to engage visitors of all ages and backgrounds. These programs include guided tours, workshops, lectures, and community events that celebrate African American culture. The museum's efforts extend beyond its walls, with outreach programs that work to bring the museum's resources to schools and community centers across the region.

The Tubman Museum not only serves as a beacon of African American culture and history but also as a place of learning and inspiration for all who visit. It stands as a testament to the resilience and creativity of the African American community, making it a pivotal institution in the landscape of American cultural and historical education.

23.   Ocmulgee Mounds National Historical Park, Macon

Ocmulgee Mounds National Historical Park, located in Macon, Georgia, is a prehistoric American Indian site that has been inhabited for over 17,000 years. Covering more than 700 acres, the park preserves the ancient earthworks and a rich history of the Native American cultures that have thrived in this region.

The park is most renowned for its large earth mounds built over a thousand years ago during the Mississippian period. These mounds, used for ceremonial and religious purposes, are impressive not only in their size but also in the sophistication of their construction. The Great Temple Mound, standing at 55 feet tall, offers a panoramic view of the surrounding landscape and the Macon skyline, providing visitors a sense of the scale and the spiritual significance of these structures.

Visitors to Ocmulgee Mounds can explore the park through a network of trails that lead to various mounds, earthworks, and other archaeological features. The visitor center offers exhibits on the history of the site, including artifacts like pottery, tools, and jewelry, which illustrate the daily life and the cultural practices of the park's ancient inhabitants.

The park also features a reconstructed earth lodge with its original 1,000-year-old floor, providing a unique glimpse into the ceremonial life of the Native Americans who built and used these earthworks. This lodge is a highlight of the site, offering an immersive experience that brings historical practices to life.

Ocmulgee Mounds is not only a site of historical and archaeological significance but also a place of natural beauty. It is home to diverse ecosystems, including wetlands, forests, and fields, which support a variety of wildlife. Bird watching, particularly during migration seasons, is a popular activity, with the park's habitats attracting numerous bird species.

The park hosts the Ocmulgee Indigenous Celebration every September, one of the largest Native American gatherings in the Southeast. This event features traditional dancing, storytelling, music, and crafts, allowing visitors to experience contemporary Native American cultures while honoring the site's ancient heritage.

24.   Little White House, Warm Springs

The Little White House in Warm Springs, Georgia, holds a unique place in U.S. history as the personal retreat of Franklin D. Roosevelt, the 32nd President of the United States. Built in 1932 while he was governor of New York, prior to his presidency, the house became a haven for Roosevelt as he sought treatment for his polio in the warm spring waters of the area. Today, it stands as a historic site, meticulously preserved to offer a glimpse into Roosevelt's private life and his time in office.

The Little White House is more than just a residence; it is a piece of living history that captures a significant era in American politics. Roosevelt spent much time here during his presidency, finding solace and relief in the therapeutic waters and using the home as a base for some of his New Deal policies. The house is where he ultimately passed away in 1945, making it a poignant memorial to his impactful life and presidency.

Visitors to the Little White House can tour the modest six-room cottage, which remains much as Roosevelt left it. The home is filled with his personal belongings and furnishings from the 1930s and 1940s, including his famous "Fireside Chat" radio microphone and his custom-made wheelchair. Personal photographs and artifacts also line the walls, providing intimate insights into his day-to-day activities at the retreat.

Adjacent to the cottage, a museum and visitor center feature exhibits that chronicle Roosevelt's life and political career, with a particular focus on his battle with polio and his deep connection to Warm Springs. The exhibits include interactive displays, historical documents, and a compelling series of personal stories and artifacts that highlight his leadership during the Great Depression and World War II.

The site also includes the historic pools that first attracted Roosevelt to Warm Springs. Although no longer in use, these pools are part of the guided tours, and visitors can learn about the treatments and community of polio sufferers who came here seeking healing.

25. FDR State Park, near Warm Springs

Nestled in the rolling hills of Pine Mountain near Warm Springs, Georgia, FDR State Park is Georgia's largest state park, sprawling across over 9,000 acres. Named after President Franklin D. Roosevelt, who found solace and inspiration in this area, the park continues to offer a sanctuary of natural beauty and a plethora of recreational activities to all its visitors.

The park's most famous feature is the 23-mile Pine Mountain Trail, which offers picturesque vistas and a range of hiking opportunities through hardwood and pines forests, past waterfalls and over streams. The trail is well-maintained and marked, providing options for serious hikers as well as those looking for a leisurely stroll or a challenging backpacking adventure.

Apart from hiking, FDR State Park offers a variety of other outdoor activities. The park has two lakes—Lake Delanor and Lake Franklin—where visitors can enjoy fishing, boating, and swimming. Several picnic areas and playgrounds make the park an ideal spot for family gatherings or a peaceful afternoon by the water.

For those who wish to extend their stay, the park boasts over 140 campsites, including fully-equipped cottages and modern campgrounds that cater to both tents and RVs. The campgrounds are beautifully integrated into the natural surroundings, offering a perfect blend of comfort and wilderness experience.

The park also reflects its historical significance with several structures built by the Civilian Conservation Corps (CCC) during the Great Depression, including stone cabins and bridges, which add to the rustic charm of the landscape. The Liberty Bell Pool, another CCC project, is a unique swimming pool shaped like a Liberty Bell, fed by cool springs.

FDR State Park also provides educational programs and guided tours that focus on the park's flora, fauna, and history. These programs are designed to enhance the visitor experience and provide insights into the area's natural and cultural heritage.

Offering a mix of breathtaking scenery, history, and ample recreational opportunities, FDR State Park is a treasure of the Georgia State Parks system, providing a glimpse into the natural world that so inspired one of America's most notable leaders.

26. Callaway Gardens, Pine Mountain

Callaway Gardens, located in Pine Mountain, Georgia, is a sprawling 6,500-acre resort complex that offers a blend of natural beauty, relaxation, and recreational activities. Founded in 1952 by Cason and Virginia Hand Callaway to promote and protect native azalea species, Callaway Gardens has evolved into a family-friendly destination with a wide range of attractions and activities.

At the heart of Callaway Gardens is the Cecil B. Day Butterfly Center, one of North America's largest tropical butterfly conservatories. This glass-enclosed habitat is home to thousands of butterflies from around the world, fluttering amongst lush tropical plants. The center not only provides a magical experience for visitors but also plays a role in butterfly conservation and education.

Another highlight is the Callaway Brothers Azalea Bowl, which showcases over 3,000 azalea plants that burst into a riot of colors each spring. The garden's landscape design enhances the natural beauty of the blooms and invites visitors to stroll along its paths to experience the full glory of the season.

For those interested in outdoor activities, Callaway Gardens offers a full spectrum of options. The gardens feature two 18-hole golf courses, more than ten miles of biking trails, and a large lake for fishing and boating. During the summer, Robin Lake Beach provides a sandy beach and watersports facilities, including paddleboarding and waterskiing.

In addition to its natural and recreational offerings, Callaway Gardens hosts a variety of seasonal events that draw visitors year-round. These include a spectacular holiday light display, a hot air balloon festival, and a series of musical concerts held in the beautiful outdoor setting of the gardens.

For accommodations, Callaway Gardens offers a range of options from a luxury spa and resort to quaint cottages and a modern campground, making it ideal for weekend getaways or extended vacations.

Made in the USA
Columbia, SC
28 November 2024